Nature's Power

Gary Price

Copyright© 2021

All Rights Reserved

Table of Contents

Dedication i
Acknowledgment ii
About the Author iii
Foreword iv
Chapter 1: My Beginnings 1
Chapter 2: Secondary School 18
Chapter 3: Football Dreams 27
Chapter 4: Girls vs Football 38
Chapter 5: New Directions 46
Chapter 6: The Start of an Incredible Journey 53
Chapter 7: The Training 69
Chapter 8: Dreams and Will 75
Chapter 9: The Greatness in Every Child 89
Chapter 10: Your Partner 95
Chapter 11: The Crab Basket 100
Chapter 12: Leave a Legacy for Yourself 104
Chapter 13: Let's Wrap It Up 112

Dedication

This book is dedicated to my soul mate and my best mate, Julie Ann Price.

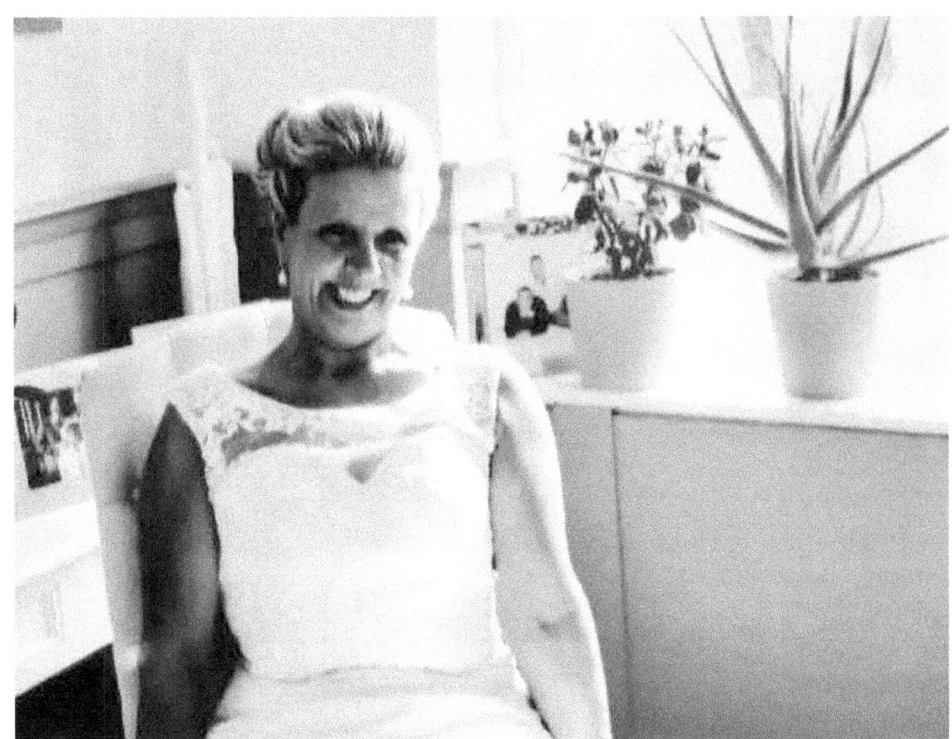

Acknowledgement

I have to start by thanking my lovely wife, Julie Ann. I could not have written this book without her aid. From reading early drafts to giving me advice on the cover and helping me edit, she was as important to this book getting done as I was. Thank you so much, dear.

About the Author

Gary Price is a London-born Cockney lad who has seen an upbringing filled with both humour and hell. He grit through sufferings such as asthma, dyslexia, bullying since he was a little child. Despite the negatives he has experienced in life, he chooses and preaches optimism to himself as well as to others. He owes his negative and positive influencers both, all of whom had a hand in teaching him valuable life lessons.

He has discovered the magical Nature's Power that resides within all and wishes to uncover it for his readers through the narration of his life's story.

Foreword

Together, we are going on a journey. At the end of this journey, you will understand the power, the strangest secret, that we all have and all use. You will begin to understand, and if I can do it, you can too. I will give everyone hope. I will give you hints along the way on this journey, so you can discover and find the secret power for yourself, within yourself.

Feel free to make notes on these pages, underline, highlight and dog-ear whenever you read anything that makes you stop and think about something. Then, any time you want to pick up this book again, you can go straight to the parts that resonated with you and read through them again.

Come on this journey with me and discover the power that's already within you.

Chapter 1: My Beginnings

Everything is energy. You are a magnet. Your power is in your thoughts.

I am an East Londoner, was born in Commercial Road under Bow Bells, which makes me a Cockney lad. As soon as you hear my voice, you'll know it. The dialect is unmistakable.

The first house I remember living in was the one my mum and dad had rented in Burlington Gardens, Chadwell Heath, with Uncle Bill and Auntie Kit. We used to live in the upper storey. They lived downstairs.

All five of us shifted to Wickford in Essex in 1955. Mum and Dad bought a bungalow, and so did Uncle Bill and Auntie Kit. They bought the house behind us.

I was two years old at the time. This is the age at which your mind begins to develop when the parents teach their kids how to speak and encourage them to walk.

You see, in my infancy days, I didn't get that parental teaching and encouragement. Can you imagine your dad saying after the first fall, "Right, that's it, sit on your arse for the rest of your life!"? Mine did. I do not know of any other parent who did.

I've discovered that babies have two fears - falling and loud noises. Babies will fall, get up and go again. That's the pattern: Fall, get up, fall, get up. They will not give in until they, at last, learn to walk. Nature's Power is there for everyone in abundance. Every being has it. It's just sometimes we may need a push for it to work. Sometimes that push may never come. In fact, others may do things to deplete our power, to the point that we begin using Nature's Power against ourselves.

On the journey we take in this book, I will reveal how you may end up working against yourself and how others influence or encourage you to by trying to keep you from being happy.

Between the ages of two and three, we are very open to the world because we are observing and learning about our habitat. It's like we are a sponge, absorbing any and everything. We take everything in, including the throw-away thoughtless comments that adults make, especially parents.

They do not know what they are doing. They are using the power. Like my dad, he gave me a nickname that he used throughout my childhood. He called me "Knob" because I used to be slight and weakly. It didn't give me a lot of confidence, for I was the smallest in my class and had the biggest ears.

I had family around me - Auntie Kit, Uncle Bill, as I've mentioned, and also Uncle Stan and Auntie Olive. The latter two also lived in Wickford. So Christmas was great. My mum was the life of our family, the party girl, always laughing. She showed me time and time again how to have fun in life just in the way she lived.

I didn't see my dad for about five years despite both of us living in the same house. He would go to work early every day before I woke up, and by the time he was back, I was in bed. He did not avoid me deliberately. He was just serious about his work. I owe it to my dad and his lifestyle, for he taught me the value of work ethic. You see, people follow those who practice what they preach, not those who give suggestions they themselves do not follow. You must walk the walk, not talk the talk. If you want your children to become successful, you must become successful first. That's leadership by example.

I eventually realised that Dad worked all the time because idleness made him grumpy. He was somewhat of a workaholic.

On the weekend days that he did not work, he would spend time with his rabbits. If I wanted to spend time with my dad, I had to be there in his shed with the rabbits. One day, I was with him when this rabbit bit his hand. Given the sense of humour I possessed (I must have inherited it from Mum), I couldn't stop laughing till he said, "Fuck off Knob, and go back in the house." That made me cry.

I was still crying when once inside I told Mum what had happened. To my surprise, Mum herself rolled up laughing. So yeah, I definitely inherited my mother's sense of humour. I used to think my dad didn't have a funny bone, but I eventually discovered that I was wrong.

I also found out that young parents have great pressure on them. Money is a big worry since they have not had that many years to save it. That's why they end up working long hours like my parents did, which consequently gives them burnout. It's the exhaustion talking when parents pass those throw-away comments like:

"You're an idiot."

"Do not go out like that, or you will get a cold."

"Don't go there. You'll drown!"

"Zip it. You don't know what you're talking about."

"You are so clumsy."

"If you get wet feet, you will catch a cold."

The list could go on.

I remember the day where I was in the pushchair, Mum was pushing me up the hill, and it was pissing down. Mum was soaking wet. I was in the pushchair, dry and comfortable, being pushed and pretending to be asleep. There's no greater and more comfortable feeling than that if you're a child. Because see, if Mum knew I was awake, she would have made me walk. I'm sure you have pretended to be asleep in the back seat and enjoyed the perks of Dad or Mum carry you in too.

As you can see, though they had some problematic traits, I was lucky with the parents I had. I feel for those children who have been mentally and physically abused. But what I'm trying to show here is that even under caring and nice parents, you still develop fears and limitations.

One example comes to mind. There was a time when my dad was having problems with moles in the garden. He bought some mole traps and placed them carefully. I thought I heard one of the traps ping in the middle of the night. Early in the morning, I ran excitedly into Dad's bedroom. "Dad! You've caught a mole. I heard it last night!" I said.

"Rubbish!" replied Dad, "You can't hear that." This is not the bad part. Saying that, he got up, and I followed, and to his surprise, a mole was caught in the trap! I jumped with joy and excitement that the mole was actually caught. But this glee turned into horror when Dad drowned the mole in the birdbath right in front of me. It upset me all day.

The thing is, I had never heard the mole trap go. I had just gone to bed repeatedly, saying to myself, "We are going to catch a mole," until I went to sleep. Children do not know about Nature's Power, but nature helps them use it intuitively.

On another occasion, my dad was building a greenhouse. One of the glass panes broke while he was putting it in, which left a long sharp shard to jut out. He placed the piece of broken pane inside the greenhouse, diagonally standing it, and told me to keep away. Mum brought him a cup of tea. He took it and sat himself down to drink the tea. He sat right where he had placed the shard, and the sharp piece of the broken pane went straight into his bum. He jumped up and said, "Fuck that!"

I had to run off before he could see me laughing.

I later went into the bathroom after recovering to find my dad bent over the bath with an inch-long cut on his backside. Blood was pouring, and Mum was wiping it. I looked at her, and she had tears of laughter in her eyes, was trying to hold it in and giving me a sign not to laugh either. But I couldn't help it. I broke into a laugh, and Dad noticed me and shouted, "Get that weirdo out of here!"

My mum was so much fun. We just laughed so much all the time.

Starting School

Aged four-and-a-half, I started school. I still live only two hundred yards away from my first school. As I mentioned, I was the smallest child with the biggest ears. That earned me the nickname Big Ears in primary school. How that helped my confidence!

At this age, I started to develop an interest in football. I would keep a small ball with me at all times. There was a football ground opposite our house. I spent most of my day every day there.

We kids were free to go to the park on our own back in the day. At age five, I used to go to school on my own and walked back home on my own - with my friends, of course.

Another lesson on Nature's Power was awaiting me. A good friend of mine was walking on the opposite sidewalk, and I ran across the main road towards him.

When I got to the middle of the road, something made me stop. Right then, a car flew past me and just brushing the front of my coat. What made me stop was the sound of people screaming and shouting.

I was shocked at what I had done and went home very quietly, reflecting on what had just happened. The effect was the same as when we trapped the mole. Nature's Power gives you clues throughout your life, and you can use that power for or against yourself. You will for sure use it, though, believe me.

Another learning experience for me came with my mum getting a job at a flower nursery. In the summer holidays, I used to go there with her. Two other children used to be there, and what incredible times we all shared. Acres were spread out before us where we played, and it seemed like the sun was out all the time. It may be odd, but I've found out when you are having a good time, you remember the sun. When you have bad times, you don't remember the sun.

A hooter used to go off at the nursery that was for tea and lunch breaks. We all used to meet in the same greenhouse to have our lunch. I could never sit with my mum, though, because she had to sit next to Len, who was another worker at the nursery.

Len once bought my mum a gold bracelet for Christmas. That gesture made shit hit the fan back at our place. Dad and Mum argued for hours, and they had forgotten I was still up and standing in the hallway, looking at a mirror. I still have that mirror today in my hallway. Looking at it always reminds me of that night, especially the moment when Dad came up to me and said, "You'd better decide which one of us you are going to live with." My world at the age of five crashed.

Moments like these in your growing life stop you from using positive power. You're filled with just the negative. And it is things like things that shape a child's mind.

The next thing I remember is that the whole family was moving down the road to this big old house with land. This is the house I still live in today. Mum went back to working at the nursery. Len stopped working there.

My dad's dream was to have a large space for land so that he could keep horses. That was his big dream, and he accomplished it because he desired and pictured it long enough and consistently enough. If you hold a picture in your mind long enough, it always materialises. Didn't the bible also say:

As a man thinketh, so is he.

That's one of the secrets of Nature's Power, which my dad had used unknowingly.

I do not remember the time from age five to seven. But during these years, I developed a stutter. So, the way the equation stands, at age seven, I'm the smallest kid with the big ears, and now I have a stutter too. It is at this age with this context that I started junior school, which did not help, to say the least. The kids at junior school can be evil, in case you didn't know that already.

Meanwhile, our household was soon back to normal with another summer holiday with Mum at the nursery.

I learned another valuable lesson when one of the men at the nursery locked me in one of the greenhouses, just for laughs. A big sliding bolt outside did the job.

For the whole hour that I was trapped, I did not panic. I just gently kicked and kept kicking the bottom of the door until the vibrations made the bolt slide out of position. I escaped, ran up to the man that had locked me, and said to him, "I'm out!" He couldn't believe it.

"How did you get out?" he said, and I told him how. "You must have been constantly kept tapping, tap, tap, tap," was all that he replied.

The lesson I learned here was, if you have a very large piece of concrete to break up, you have to go through it with a Kango hammer. When you start, it seems impossible that it will ever break. But keep tapping, tap, tap, tap, and it will indeed shatter. If you use the same strategy to hammer the picture of what you want in your subconscious mind, you will obtain that desire. Be it good or bad, tap, tap, tap, and it will materialise.

Another summer holiday arrived, and this time I did not have to go with Mum. I would be down at the park, which is at the bottom of my road. You see, my school days were not the enjoyable kind, to put it mildly. I had dyslexia, although I did not know it at the time. I never learned my alphabet and do not know it to this day. So, being the smallest, having big ears, a stutter and dyslexia, I had everything going for me. I would like to add, this is a piece of cake compared to what some other kids go through.

It's no surprise why many kids never succeed in life. When they are born, as I said at the beginning, they have two fears: the fear of falling and the fear of loud noises. By the time they are five, they pick up many fears. Parents and other schoolchildren cause this with their throw-away comments.

At seven years of age, children have developed a set of patterns that prepares them for junior school days. So when I start junior school, here I am, once again, the smallest in the class got the biggest ears, stutter, dyslexia, and now I have asthma too. All these factors combined made me a very shy and timid boy. I was deadly quiet in class. I would never stand up and answer a question. My lack of confidence was compounded on the second day of the new term when a rather loud ginger boy would not stop talking. The teacher eventually threw the wooden blackboard rubber at him that struck him on the back of the head—whatever hope I had of raising my voice died right there. That event made me want to remain even quieter.

I was given many lemons in life, out of which I was going to make lemonade. To recap:

- Smallest in class
- Biggest ears
- Stutter
- Dyslexic
- Asthma
- Nickname Knob
- Things are done *for* you, not *to* you

So far, I've been pointing out all the minuses. What was on the plus side for me? I was lightning quick. Great with a ball, great in all sports. The sporting arena was where I felt comfortable. That's when I became equal or above others, which should bring to remind you:

It's not the size of the man, it's the size of the fight inside the man.

So, I started to have mates, but also foes. The ginger boy who got hit with the blackboard rubber was my bully who made life hell for me in the playground.

"Big Ears, where's your mate? Where's Noddy, Dumbo?" He would say. I had to hear this right through to senior school. I did not realise it at the time, but my bully also taught me a big lesson: how to value real ones.

I had schoolmates by this time. We would go down to the park and play football. You would meet other boys down there, maybe from other schools too. This still happens today, by the way. You have two captains and each, in turn, picks their team from our line of standing boys, including the new ones. A lot of these were two or three years older than us.

From that very first time, I used to stand there in the line with my inhaler in hand. I was the last one to be picked the first time we played. An odd number of team players broke out, and the two older captains began arguing who was going to be lumbered with Dumbo. And guess what, that was the last time that I got called that. The team I got paired with ripped our opponents apart, scoring 10 goals. One of them was the most iconic, where I flew past the entire team and scored Lionel Messi style.

So, next time down at the park, the older boys are captains. They have the first pick, and guess who gets picked first? Yeah, you know it's Dumbo! It was amazing how nobody had wanted Dumbo a few days ago. That day, the head boy was left saying, "Fuck knows how he can run so fast with those ears!" So, keep the reminder in mind:

Every child has been born with a gift, but most die with the music still in them.

By this age, I had never seen a film and couldn't read either. At home, we had gotten our first black and white TV. It was always when I was in bed that my dad would turn the TV on. If I was lucky enough to be in the lounge, the TV would only show those gardening or horse programmes. I always found that very weird.

It turned out that I did not need to watch TV to develop my imagination. For instance, at school, we were asked to do a project of making anything out of paper or wood. This was my first year at junior school, and what did I make out of cardboard? I made a pyramid and used pipe cleaners to make little people, pulling the large stones. Now where the fuck did that come from? No idea. To me, it was no big deal, but the teachers could not believe me when I said I had not ever watched TV. Strange, right?

When I was eight, my dad took me to my first football game: Spurs v Liverpool. I was so excited it gave me asthma, but nothing was going to stop me from going.

In the past, I had bad luck with exciting moments. Like when Mum organised a birthday party for me, and I ended up in bed with asthma while everyone was in the lounge enjoying my party without me! So come hell or high water, I was going to this game. As the saying goes:

If the dream is big enough, the facts don't count.

The sheer excitement I felt as I first saw my first pitch in a stadium! At 6:03 pm in this game, I found my first hero - Peter Thompson, Liverpool's left-winger. How he took nice-one-Cyril Knowles to the cleaners! Liverpool won two-nil, and Peter Thompson became my idol. I copied the way he played, and it was he who made me a Liverpool supporter for life.

Now my junior school days were made. I had unlocked some sort of inner power. We always had school dinners in the dining hall with all our friends gathered. I was starting to find that I could make people laugh. On one occasion, I made my mate laugh so hard, he choked and sneezed in my blancmange. I was not going to eat that now, so I pushed the plate away.

The headteacher saw me push it and said, "Price, why are you not eating your dessert?"

"I don't want it now," I told her.

She replied: "You take it and eat it."

"No," I said.

She replied, "Do you realise how many people are starving in Africa?" I looked at her and said politely, "Then please, Miss, give my dessert to them."

She went red in the face, with anger, I think, and sent me to the headmaster. I faced the music confidently.

Nature's Power gives kids clues how to have a strong will.

So, by then, I was a young boy:
- Smallest in the class
- Biggest ears

- Stutter
- Dyslexic
- Asthma
- Nickname Knob (but no one knew that in my earliest years.)
- Was fast
- Good at all sports, especially football

My junior school days were great. I got into the school team as a 3rd-year pupil, when it was only for 4th-year pupils, and ran the sixty metres for the school. By the 4th year, I was playing for the school team, the District and the County, three football games a week. Games in those days took place during school time.

In the summer, I was in the gymnastics team. The 3rd and 4th years at junior school were even more superb. I was very rarely attending lessons, but the sport was life. I still had that ginger prick Billy Buckhorn bullying me. I did not pay much attention to it, for I had learned early on to remove all human ticks out of my life.

In those days, each of us had bottles of milk at the morning break, and, I suppose from the money that Dad's work ethic brought home, I got my mum to buy me a big box of Nesquik, which was a flavouring you put in the milk. I had chocolate and a banana. No sooner, I had boys lining up by my desk, and I was selling a spoonful of Nesquik for a threepenny bit. That entrepreneurial project lasted for about twelve weeks until I got caught and told by the headmaster, "You can't earn money in school hours."

At the end of my last year, I won the Sportsboy of the Year award and received a trophy and a book together with a glowing speech from the headmaster, as we were the first boys from that school to represent the school in the District and County teams. My good friend Alfie was with me all the way.

I got home that night very proud and excited, waiting for my dad to come home. I told him about my day and showed him the trophy and the book. I told him what the headteacher had said. You see, when we had those football matches at school, all the kids used to watch, and parents would also be there. But my dad never saw me play in those days. I wanted to show him I was good at something.

He let me finish, then said, "That's great, Knob." He opened the sportsbook and said, "Read it."

I could not read the first three words.

"Great," he said, "Sportsboy of the Year and can't fucking read. What a waste of four years." Well, that was my dad.

I didn't know how to make anyone believe that sports made me feel alive in the truest sense. While I was playing football, I didn't stutter, and the asthma was clear during the game. We had a dog at home that I used to talk to, and I noticed I did not stutter when I would talk to the dog. The problem with that was the words would be "B-b-b-bah wow!"

I couldn't do anything about my height or my big ears. Those were genetics, but everything else was a result of a lack of confidence. These things were given *for* me, not *to* me.

Nature's Power gives clues to children. It depends on parents, peers, teachers to pave the way for them. But how much they knock out of these kids through thought-less words!

Today I speak with people who can't remember their school days or early years. I can remember back to when I was two. So I wonder what went wrong for those kids?

For me, those early years over at the park were fab. My mum had a full-time job, and my dad worked all hours. Mum used to make my breakfast before she left. Dinner was served when I got home from the park.

Fifteen or twenty of us would be at the park. We'd pick sides, put jumpers down as goalposts and play all morning. We'd score the winning goal, go home and have the dinner which Mum made for me. Then we would go back down the park again, return to have tea, dress up in black clothes, go back down the park to the woods and play runouts in the dark. That was the life. I feel so sorry for kids today who can't do that because everyone knows the perverts are out there. You can't blame the parents trying to keep their kids safe… or can you?

Even back in those days over at the park, the perverts still lurked. We somehow knew that but had no fear because we could handle them, take the piss and run. Let's put it this way. No one was ever going to catch me at the very least.

I remember the Christmas when my house in Mount Road was getting rebuilt. They were clearing the land, and my family and I were left sitting freezing cold on cement bags, eating our Christmas dinner with no ceilings.

Dad was still at the job all week while his weekends were spent working on the house. I worked with him, helping him to clear the land. I used to get half-a-crown for my labour. In those days, that was my only source of pocket money.

Is that really a bad thing?

I don't hesitate in saying that life in those days was great. I had friends who lived near my house, like next door and opposite our lane. Five of my mates, in fact, all lived on the same road, and all were three years older than me. They looked after me, taught me about things and were "Herberts".

On one particularly freezing cold day, we had no heating. All the sirens were going off, and there were heavy clouds of smoke in the air. We all rushed down through the park to the High Street to see this huge wooden building that housed a builders' merchant and a lawnmower shop completely ablaze. I think the whole of Wickford was there watching. The heat was wonderful, the fire destructive. Out of every adversity, there is some seed of benefit.

Weird things happened at High Street sometimes. Like the day when a bull had escaped from the slaughterhouse there. He started running up and down the street and going in shops. People were chasing this poor thing, trying to catch it.

Policemen and firemen were all there. What fun that was. How very unfortunate for the bull that he got caught in the butcher's shop.

We used to go out at night and walk around the streets playing Knock Down Ginger. It was a running game. I loved that because despite my mates being three years older than me, I was still the fastest. We would walk around with small wet lumps of clay and throw them at the front window of the house, so it would stick. I only did this once.

We all got our clay, and as I was the youngest, I got the last turn to throw. By the time my turn came, that clay had probably been in my hand for an hour, and naturally, it had gone hard. It was my turn, and my target was a lovely, big dining room window. I threw it, a perfect shot, but to my shock, it went straight through the window, net curtain and onto the dining table, where the family were eating their meal. In a flash, I ran down Wick Lane into Mount Road and home.

The man of the house rushed out and caught two of my mates. They said they knew nothing about it. One hour later, a policeman knocked on my door (something would not happen today). Dad answered, and I hid in the airing cupboard. Dad left with the officers and went to see the man who owned the house whose window I'd smashed. Dad apologised on my behalf and said he would replace the window and pay for any other damages.

To my surprise, Dad told me the man was laughing in response. He'd said, "I ran out and saw this little bullet disappearing down Mount Road. I went to my daughter's Sports Day the other week where I had seen this little lad run. When I saw that little bullet run down Mount Road again today, I knew there's only one person who can run like that - Gary Price."

So, bang went my pocket money for the next 8 weeks and remember, I only got pocket money when I worked.

Anyway, I think this was around the time when the Council was widening the river down at the bottom of my road because Wickford got flooded a few years back. There was a concrete wall from the roadside down to the top of the riverbank, about fifteen feet high. At the bottom, the riverbed was concreted with reinforcing rods sticking up out of it. They must have been twelve inches high and twelve inches apart. I slipped down that wall and fell onto the reinforcing rods—no serious injury.

My mate did not know, so he ran back up the road screaming into his house, saying, "Gary's dead!" His mum and some neighbours came running out and down the road to find me walking up to meet them. I had fallen onto these rods, but I fell in between them. Thankfully, nothing pierced me. It's just that one rod went through the front of my jumper and another through the back of my jumper. I said to Paul's mum, "My mum's going to kill me. She's just knitted this!"

But there was no killing involved, of course. I will say that I laid in bed that night, reflecting on how I had been saved from the rods. I started getting flashbacks of infant days when I had run across the road and just missed the car, and another time, months earlier when Dad had said I could build a bonfire in the field for Fireworks Night, and I had to get the wood.

Off I had gone down to the river to fetch the wood. The river was really high and flowing fast, and a big log came floating down. I made a grab for it but slipped. Splash! I went under the water and grabbed the log as the water dragged me down the river. Then I grabbed a tuft of grass on the bank and pulled myself out.

I couldn't swim, but I didn't drown either.

Use these examples to remind you that Nature's Power is in the subconscious mind. It will always direct you and save you if you use it the right way. Nature lets kids use it in the right way, but when we become adults, we choose.

Joke

A nursery teacher says to her class, "Who can give me a sentence with 'definitely' in it?"

Sally stands up and says, "The sky is definitely blue."

"Sorry," said the teacher, "the sky is sometimes grey."

Julie stands up and says, "The trees are definitely green."

"Sorry," said the teacher, "the trees are sometimes brown in winter."

Bertie stands up and says, "Miss, are there lumps in a fart?"

Not amused, the teacher says harshly, "No, Bertie, that is not what is asked for. I want a sentence with 'definitely' in it."

"Oh good," says Bertie, "I have definitely shit myself then."

Your Notes

Chapter 2: Secondary School

The decisions we make determine our future.

My dad had, back in the day, taught me how to shoot a weapon and how to go about building things. I could thus contribute to the construction process during the rebuilding of my home.

About the weapons, though, we had about six guns: one shotgun, which Dad kept locked away in his gun safe, and the other two were air rifles. Dad told me I could use the guns when I was by myself only; it was not allowed when my mates were around. I ended up disobeying him.

The first time my mates came around the house, we brought the guns out in the field. One second we were playing around, the next, I ended up shooting my mate in the foot. His mum came around to complain. My dad didn't say anything, but I found all the guns smashed in the dustbin the next morning.

Time went on, and the day arrived for my first day at senior school. I was 11. The thing about senior school is that the day you walk in, the big lads right there, fishing for the boys they are going to stick in the dustbin. I had to avoid being one of their targets.

We found out our classes, and as usual, I was in the bottom class.

Our teacher's name was Mrs Rose, and she was four feet tall. This woman, without a doubt, changed my life. Only second day in, Mrs Rose came up to me and said the most incredible words:

"Price, I know all about you. You should not be in my class. You're going to start working, living to your potential. There is no football during school hours. After school and Saturday mornings, that's when football is played in this school. At the end of the year, you will finish top and go up a level."

What was funny with that was that I actually believed everything she said. She would say to me, "Price - ain't ain't a word." That year, I finished top in spelling and second overall. I went up a level the next year. Believe it or not, from then on out, I went up every year. It all began with a suggestion that, coupled with belief, gave me another important lesson in life:

Suggestion with belief is the most powerful thing on this Earth.

Now it's my opinion that my childhood is quite normal, regardless of how it may seem to you. And as I have said, Nature's Power helps the children profoundly. However, sadly there are abused children in whom Nature's Power subsides because their subconscious mind does not recover from the shock of what the adults have done to them.

I was very fortunate to have found Mrs Rose. What a wonderful teacher she was, and pretty fashionable too. She wore a ring on every finger. Her pet peeve was students running through the school. She told every pupil not to run. So many times, I saw Mrs Rose walking around a corner with her arm out straight, fist closed, the rings on every finger blinging, with boys running into her fist then onto the floor spitting blood. Mrs Rose would simply look at them on the floor and say, "Walk - don't run."

Every teacher in that school was a piece of work, a wide range of characters. I compare that with today, and it's so apparent that the contemporary world of teaching is so different. I think most of the teachers at my school of then would probably be banned today.

Mrs Rose has remained my favourite. This was the first teacher who told me I could do something with my brain. That year, I came first in spelling. I couldn't secure the top position in the class that year, but I came second, and I moved up the next year.

Thanks to her, I had built my foundation academically too. She showed me that words can be so powerful. If you tell someone with belief and sincerity that they can reach the stars, then even if they only hit the moon, they have succeeded.

As for sports, football games took place after school and on Saturday mornings. After our first training session, I got straight into the school team. One of our sports teachers was a huge man named Mr Jones who taught rugby.

I remember a games lesson in the very early days. It was really muddy on the sports ground, and he was teaching us rugby. As you can imagine, we were filthy with mud all over us at the end of the game. We all went back into the changing rooms, undressed, and into a huge shower room, we went. We were all in there under the showers when we heard Mr Jones shouting, "… In every class, there is always a fat boy." He was speaking to a boy who was standing there naked but refusing to get into the shower.

Mr Jones continued, "Look, Richardson, I can't have you smelling in your next lesson. You, my friend, are having a shower." Richardson refused again, and Mr Jones grabbed him by the cock and pulled Richardson into the shower. To us, it was very funny. Richardson was on tiptoes screaming, and Jonesey (as we called our teacher) was marching through the shower with Richardson's cock in his hand!

This is what I meant when I said the teachers of our time would be banned today. I don't think Jonesey could have gotten away with that today. But he taught Richardson an enduring lesson. He never refused to get in the shower again after that, and all of us knew not to say no to Mr Jones.

Another man named Mr Collier, who ran the tuck shop, was a complete nutter. He would grab the window blinds, twist them into a knot and then tell two of us to straighten them out. He would throw big boxes of crisps at us. He would randomly get someone up to read a passage of a book. You would stand up and read two words, and he would shout, "That's enough, sit down." Hence, a complete nutter.

We walked into a class one day, and everywhere were huge books. They must have been six inches thick - the very definition of heavy. He said to us, "Right. Your assignment for today is to deliver these books to every teacher in the school. Price, this is your book - go and deliver yours to Mrs Smith." He never told us where these teachers were. I mean, this school was huge. I was out two hours or more looking for Mrs Smith. I asked other teachers, "Do you know where I can find Mrs Smith?" But no luck.

I looked everywhere for this teacher, walking around with my arms laden and stretched out in front of me. I was dreading going back to Mr Collier with the book still in hand. Having failed, as I walked back into the classroom, he was shouting at another boy, saying, "You have not been trying hard enough. Do not come back here until you find Mr Balance."

Mr Balance was the metalwork teacher, a very funny man who wasn't shy to use and teach colourful language to the boys. I wished right then that I had Mr Balance's book, as I knew where he was. So I heard all this shouting and shit myself because I was next.

Fearing the worst, I confessed to Mr Collier, "I can't find Mrs Smith." He replied in a loud voice, "I know Price, she's not in today!" laughed and took the book off me.

We also had Mr Silvey. He was the art teacher. A lovely man, but also a frail man. And kids can be so nasty with such teachers. They used to lock him in his art room and abuse him terribly.

One day, he was speaking about the Mona Lisa painting and said that no other artist who copied the painting had been able to produce the same smile that da Vinci did. "I have tried my version," he told us, "and I would like to show you my painting of the Mona Lisa." He went into his cupboard, brought out the painting and stood it on the easel. To me, it looked fabulous, but half the class just laughed and shouted that it was useless. Poor Mr Silvey, he took it to heart, went dejected back into his cupboard and cried.

Mr Barnes was 6'7" tall and taught us music. This was the kind of teacher you did not mess around with. I'll tell you why.

Back in those days, we had a shop down the road called Pollards, and they had black plimsolls with a grey sole. Mr Barnes had cut the sole off a size 13 plimsolls, which he called 'Horace'. We did not know about that… yet.

So my mate Dougie and I got caught talking and laughing in his lesson. He shouted at Dougie and me, "Price, Bull, see me after this lesson."

We stayed back after the lesson, and he pulled Horace out of the drawer. With chalk, he wrote the name "Horace" on the blackboard, drew a face with a drooping mouth and wrote the word "face." He said, "So Price, you have two options, 5,000 lines or Horace." I told him I would have Horace.

He said, "Bull, what's your choice?"

Horace," said Bull.

"Great," he replied (I think Barnesy preferred this option). We all wore black trousers as school uniform.

"Okay, Price, bend over." I heard a swish and this grey rubber sole went all across my arse. It was one of those pains that make the hairs on the back of your neck stand up, making you shiver with the pain. Dougie could see the pain on my face and promptly said to Mr Barnes, "I think I will have the 5,000 lines, Sir." Mr Barnes, with a wry smile, said, "Bully, for that, you now can have both. Bend over." And he did have both; for some reason, that tickled me.

That was just a few of this motley crew of teachers. With these as a reference, I wonder the same thing again: would these teachers have jobs today? Did they traumatise us? Were they bad for us? I honestly don't think so. They taught us about life and common sense. Maybe back in the day, we may have dreaded these figures, but they did more good to us than bad. They were like our hot water, you know like they say:

Your future is like a teabag: not worth much until you go through hot water.

So, after I had started in this school, a new sports teacher arrived, Mr Cowgill. He was the first teacher I had a conflict with. He led the next rugby training session. As I normally did, I went past the fullback and delivered a perfect cross.

Mr Cowgill stopped the game. "Price," he called out, "I don't want you to go past the fullback and deliver the cross as before. Most times, the fullback will tackle you, and you can't deliver. Let me show you. Right, I'm the fullback, and I will stop you."

So, I picked up the ball, ran towards him and I could see he wanted me badly. I went one way, then the other, and pushed the ball through his legs. That's what we call a 'nutmeg', and you shouted it at the same time you did it, which meant you it was on purpose, and meant humiliation for the opponent. Through his legs, the ball went, and I was around him and away and delivered the cross into the box. For that, he dropped me out of the school team for six weeks - it straight up broke my heart.

The two of us never got on after that for all the remaining school years. Our paths crossed later on a few occasions after I left school, but we never made up. I remember when I was leaving school to join West Ham or Chelsea, he said to me, "You will never be a pro footballer." But I never let his or anyone else's opinion determine my future.

Still, these teachers taught me so many valuable lessons that kids today don't get. In my opinion, the schools are so concerned about their ratings and money that they forget about the children. I firmly believe you should teach them how to spell, add up, read and write. But you should also especially concentrate then on finding and honing their gifts because every human has one. When a child has a dream, he or she learns how to achieve that, but he needs to be given the opportunity. Teach the kids cooking, gardening and about vegetables, the practical things of life which are getting lost today. Each contains some value for Nature's Power within us. It seems to me today it's merely about ticking boxes, and common sense is not common.

Thanks to all my tuitions and training, the day came when I left school with the offer of two trials, one with West Ham and the other with Chelsea. The dream that I had been pursuing passionately was on the stove and cooking.

But I'm not someone with superpowers or something special that you do not have in you. Every human being has the power, the ability to picture a goal or a dream that, with belief and will, manifests in real life. Nothing on this planet can stop it from coming true if the desire and faith for its becoming are strong enough.

Joke

The boy was dying, and his girlfriend was beside him.

He said to his girlfriend, "I must confess before I die."

The girlfriend said, "Shush, just rest."

"No," said the boyfriend. "I must do this. I had sex with your sister, with your best friend and with your work colleague."

Girlfriend said, "I know, that is why I poisoned you."

Your Notes

Chapter 3: Football Dreams

Your future is like a teabag: not worth much until you go through hot water.

I ended up leaving school, bearing in mind I'd had a good education. I encountered weird teachers, yes, but the best thing they taught me was common sense. Along this time, my head had started to grow, and so my ears didn't look big anymore. I no longer stutter, although my dog did.

I was still a shy boy, but always happy, always laughing, and that was due to my mum. I was still small also, but muscles started growing in my shoulders, chest, arms and legs. It was evidence that Nature always works in ways to compensate. I was small but very strong.

Remember my bully Billy Buckhorn in the second year? One day he started on me, and I ended up hitting him in the stomach, then as he bent over, I grabbed the top of his hair and landed two uppercuts into his nose. He was there on his arse, pleading with me to stop. This was on the playing field with everyone watching. Other kids, who were also bullied by Buckhorn, were cheering.

Half an hour later, after the beating, Billy Buckhorn came up to me and said, "Gary, why didn't you do that years ago? I would have left you alone!" We were mates after that. And this should serve as a lesson for you out there: if you don't stand up for yourself, you will fall for everything.

As for my intellectual capacities, I was still dyslexic, but nobody recognised that condition in those days. I had asthma, but that never stopped me.

So, let's reflect on what we've explored so far: by the time you are seven, negative thoughts and fears are hardwired in your brain. Senior school can add to these or unlock them. Nature's Power, in which I believe, gives you clues and offers help to the child who has an average childhood and good parents. Abused children have to start a long way back, but with self-belief, anyone can turn things around. It doesn't matter how old you are.

When you become a teenager, Nature stops giving you clues. From then on, you and every single person in this world uses Nature's Power, this secret, God, or whatever you all like to call it.

You use it for you or against you, but you will use it.

The strangest secret of the universe is so simple: picture what you want, hold the picture in your mind long enough, and what you want will happen.

So, what makes it hard? Here's a list of few things:

1. The negative thoughts hardwired into your subconscious, which starts from around the age of two
2. Your partner, husband or wife
3. The Crab Basket
4. Sex

I will cover each one of these as we carry on this journey together.

***

Here we go, full steam ahead. My football trials were three months away after I left school. At fifteen, I went on my first "mates" holiday on a coach to Yarmouth. I discovered beer, and every time I spoke to a girl, I had stiffening in the loins.

All my school days, especially through senior school, I had had no interest in girls since I thought who was going to talk to the smallest in the class with the biggest ears? Hence, the stiffening consequence.

What a treat that holiday was. Beer and the small head were taking control of the big head, which means the bell-end was overriding the brain.

This is number 4 on the list above - if you never get control of the sexual urge, you will spend five decades of your life failing. I will cover this later on. But at fifteen and through your teenage years - experiencing heightened sexuality is normal.

As for back at home, the house was constructed. We had stables at the bottom of the garden with horses and dogs. I was going to work with my dad and finding out more about him. Keep in mind up to this point, I hadn't known my dad had a sense of humour. I realised he was a bloody funny man.

I went to work with dad and helped him with the horses. That wasn't my dream, but he taught me so much about work, the countryside and the animal world.

I was sixteen by this time, the age where we boys think we can rule the world. We find beer and girls, and we know it all. I even say to my son, "You're sixteen, and you might as well leave home now because you know it all."

My mates were all taller than me, but I was built like a brick shithouse with sideburns. We would go into the Castle, and I would fetch the beers because I was the only one they would serve. I got a new nickname, "Gazza." At that time, only one of the team knew the nickname my dad had given to me. He'd heard my dad call me Knob at home. He asked, "Why does your dad call you Knob?" and I told him, "I have to uncurl out of my pants." He laughed and said, "Yeah, right," but it nailed that nickname.

One Friday night, Dad said we were going to work on Saturday morning, and he was taking his gun. We had a big Bedford Dormobile van, in which we picked up his mate John the next morning. I was in the back on the wheel arch, with the tools and the gun. We were heading out to a place called Burnham-on-Crouch.

We were driving through the country lanes, and Dad said, "Just up here, there's a field full of partridges. Load the gun, Knob," which I did. We slowed up and then stopped. John had the gun set on the edge of the open window. The partridges started to run through a hole in the hedge. Dad shouted to John, "Fucking aim at that hole in the hedge!" which he did with both barrels. We had about a minute before the farmer came out of his house after us.

Dad said, "Go and pick them up quickly. Knob, go with John." I had work boots on that were too big and an oversized coat. John and I struggled over the fence, picking up these partridges. I kept falling over my boots, rushing about picking up these birds. We had arms full of them. Rushing back over the fence with the farmer in hot pursuit, we threw the birds in the back of the van and sped off.

I was in the back of the van with about twenty half-dead birds. The others were flapping about. Dad said, "Don't just sit there, fucking neck them."

Dad also taught me how to ride, so we could go out together. My mum had a horse as well, so our family could all go out together. Dad had showjumpers and hunt horses, and he had six stables that were all full.

At work, Dad had John as his labourer. Dad was a plasterer, so I helped around the site, unloading lorries and any other labour-type jobs. The men on those sites taught me so much about life and every day was a funny event. But it was all hard work too. One of my jobs was to empty the piss tins, which could almost never be done without spilling it on your boots. The horses were fun until you started the mucking out. You had to bring hay and straw bales into the barn, and with the grooming; not an easy job.

When the barn had only about ten bales left, we would have the three Jack Russells with us, which we had bred. They were in the barn with us for one reason - rats and mice. As Dad moved the last bales, they would run out, and the dogs killed them in a flash. I shat myself the first time and tied my trousers up at each ankle, so the rats didn't run up my legs.

One of our foals was a stallion, and Dad said we would keep him as a stallion and breed with him to earn some money along the way. Dad had a special horse that he had bred. He called her Country Girl, and she was going to make a very good showjumper. She used to be in stable No. 6, and the stallion was in No. 1. He was in there because we could take him around the back, ready for action.

I used to ride the stallion around the roads, calm as anything, but when we put the white head collar on him, he knew it was time for some action, and he was a different beast. Country Girl was a big horse, and the stallion, called Survival, used to look past the other mares and would always be looking at her.

We had a foal born one morning, which just did not come round. I sat with it all day and night, struggling. The vet came the next morning and put the foal down and the mother as well, which was my mum's horse. With tears in my eyes, I told Dad it had been the worst day and night of my life. To my astonishment, he cried. That was the first time I knew my dad had feelings and that he had them, especially for me. My mum broke down too. I decided I was never having another horse.

Those days soon passed, and I was back to having fun, working with Dad. After the evening, I would be out with my mates to the Youth Centre and the pub and on the hunt for girls.

The fair soon hit our town - Wickford Carnival. My mate Dave and I went down to the fair after doing the horses. There was a bloke there doing donkey rides. He had a big horse box and ten donkeys. Of course, me and Dave, who was a year older than me, could ride. The bloke who owned the donkeys could see that we could handle them. He asked if we would look after them and keep the rides going while he went for lunch in the Castle. It was about 1 o'clock, and we agreed happily.

The queue was massive, and we had two donkeys each. Giving donkey rides to people around was great fun. It got to 6 o'clock, and everyone had gone. We tied up the donkeys and checked they had hay and water, and we left them to find this guy. As we walked up to the Castle, we saw him fall out of the doorway, pissed as a fart. He couldn't stand up. We approached this fine gentleman who shouted at us, "Fuck off, you little cunts!" and so as not to aggravate him any further, we walked home.

Both of us had bulging pockets full of coins, which, when we counted them, came to £150. Thank you very much. That counts as a good day.

The next day we went to the fair was Sunday night. We were going to give the donkey owner his money, but he had gone, so we had a great time AND made some money.

We were talking to some girls, and one of them lived opposite my house. We were with them all night and went over to the park, chatting and having a laugh. The girls went home because one of the girls' dads came over and got them. We didn't have a clue what the time was by then.

Dave went one way, and I started to walk the other way up Mount Road, where my house was. As I started to walk up the road, from a long way off and in the dark, I could see what looked like a little gnome sitting on the top of the gate post. As I got nearer, I could see it was my dad.

As I walked to where he was, he said, "Where the fuck have you been? Your mother is worried sick." Now, my dad has the biggest hands you would ever see, like digger buckets. As I ran past him, his left caught me behind the head. I ran in straight to bed, and nothing else was said or done.

At that age of raging hormones, we really do feel like we can do anything. We end up using Nature's Power to the fullest in one way: girls and the chase.

The day arrived of my first football trial with West Ham. It was a Saturday morning at Chadwell Heath, West Ham's Training Ground. I was on my own and shitting myself. I was still very shy around people I didn't know. There was John Lyle, who years after became the West Ham Manager and a lovely old man called Walter "Wally" St. Pier.

We had to register, so they knew they had the right boys. I sat in the corner, getting ready with lots of big noisy lads jumping up and down getting excited. I just sat in my corner, shitting myself. Wally came up to me and said, "Relax, Gary, it will be alright. Just show us what you can do."

It was an hour-long game. Here's the rule about a trial game, everyone plays for themselves. I was out on the left-wing upfront and didn't touch the ball for the first half. In the second half, I got two balls knocked up to me, and both were in the air. A big lad was marking me, which was the last thing I needed. The ball was up in the air, and I was the smallest on the pitch. Both times this big lad headed the ball away.

Nearly an hour passes, and I'm not in the game, and I haven't said a word. I could have been upset and disappointed, but dissatisfaction and discouragement are not the absence of things but the absence of vision. And I had the fucking vision.

This was my dream! I needed the fucking ball, so I started to use my voice, which for a little bloke was loud. A couple of minutes to go, and I receive the ball on the floor. You see, I knew if I could get this ball at my feet, I would do this big fella. This is my dream. So this is what I do:

I push the ball down the side of the defender, and I go the other side… I was gone. He was looking at my small arse - I nutmegged the next one, which is a ball through the legs, swerved left past the next defender and put a cross in for the centre forward to head home, and that was the end of the trial.

I was gutted because that was the only thing I did for the whole hour. I sat in the dressing room, upset. John Lyle came and sat next to me.

"Shout more! Take on that pitch, Gary! You did nothing all the game, but in that last minute, I could see what you are all about. I want you to come training with us twice a week in the evenings, and there is a good chance we will sign you."

Can you imagine the excitement I felt? Someone believed in me. I was six feet tall.

I got home over the moon. Dad was pleased and said there were horses to muck out. That brought me down to Earth. Dad was paving my way until I decided what I was going to do. Football or plastering.

The following Saturday, I had a trial at Chelsea. We met at Stamford Bridge with the coach sitting us all down and coming out with the words: "In the last year, we have had 3,000 boys for trials, and only three have made it."

Those words alone must have wrecked 50% of those boys' dreams.

The format was different to the West Ham trial: this one had three thirty-minute halves. I came on in the second half and did absolutely nothing. I never received the ball. In the last and final half, from the kick-off, I received the ball, blasted my fullback, delivered the cross, and that gave me confidence. Because of that, I kept receiving the ball, and I tore this boy who was marking me to shreds. He had travelled down from Scotland, and I ruined this boy's dream. I felt so sorry for him.

In the end, the coach said: "I'm going to read out the names we want to come back Saturday week." The list he read out was only half the number of boys on the benches… and I was one of them. I had pictured this for years, so what hit me then euphoria. The dream was coming together.

Take this as the cue to realise that what you think about all day long is what will happen. It's hard work, but keep holding on to that picture. Don't let anyone steal your dream. Don't let anyone's opinion determine your future. They are called dream-stealers.

So, back to Earth, but with excitement, I was helping Dad with the horses. We started to breed with our stallion. My job was to lead the mare around the back. We had a big farm gate, so I had to get the mare's arse up against the gate and come around with the stallion, Survival. When the mare lifted up her tail and her minge started going like a budgie's eye, we were ready. When we were done, dad took the now calm stallion back into the stable.

I walked around the paddock with the mare. Dad came around with a bucket of freezing water and threw it up the back end of the mare. The mare charges forward after this cold water hits her minge and makes it tighten up, so it does not shit the semen out. I remember the first time I had to throw the bucket of water. I missed the horse completely and got my dad.

While I was still sixteen, my dad used to teach me to drive on an old airfield runway in Bradwell. When I was seventeen, I drove everywhere with Dad. I had two lessons and passed my test in the first go. It was easy in those days.

Another avenue opened up for us eventually. Dad had a massive manure heap, and gardeners wanted it. So, I started up my manure business. Every Sunday, I loaded up the van and delivered. A fiver a load. It was hard work and great in the winter because as you dug into the heap, it was very hot and steaming. It stank and attracted hundreds of flies on the windscreen, but it put money in my pocket.

Where there's shit, there's money, it was a funny thought for me.

By this time, me and the other footballer lads were training twice a week with West Ham. The next visit would be to Hendon, Chelsea's Youth Training Ground, which was a trek up a hill, but the most perfect place for young footballers. You could see the whole of Wembley Stadium clearly in the distance. Well, England had won the World Cup that year and every day, looking at that stadium was a dream-building session.

After that second trial, they wanted to see more of me, so I started to go to the Chelsea day sessions twice a week and to West Ham twice a week in the evening. I was still working with Dad and doing my manure run every Sunday. What lay ahead for my future was still a question mark, though I at least knew the two roads that lay before me.

Joke

Iceland now has a dating agency - a bag for life.

Your Notes

Chapter 4: Girls vs Football

You will end up with a nest egg or a goose egg. Depends on the chick you marry.

I met my first girlfriend down the Youth Centre, and we used to see each other twice a week. She was still in her last year of school. We would be boyfriend and girlfriend for a few weeks, a new experience which was, then part for a month, then come back together. This carried on for a long while - back and forth.

I saved my earnings, and me and the mates, we went back to Yarmouth in a caravan. It was a great site. They had three music venues, and we were in and out of them every night. I don't think any of us had had a sexual adventure by that time, so we were on the hunt to get lucky.

I remember a girl coming over to chat. There were six of us, and she liked being with us all. She said we were fun, and she was there with her mum. All she wanted to do was dance with me.

The second night we were dancing, she asked me to walk with her along the beach. Now, this girl was older than me and was a stunner. Lovely long hair and huge breasts. She looked amazing, plus the little head was shouting, controlling the big head. On the beach, we started kissing. She laid down, lifted up her dress and slid her knickers off. I dropped my trousers. The bell-end was as hard as I'd known; even a cat wouldn't scratch it. Then she said, "Hurry up, my boyfriend is turning up soon." So, with a fully erect bell-end, on I go, shaking, excited. Made the entrance, was in once, pulled out quickly to unload, and that was that.

We got back to the club, and her boyfriend was there. She started dancing with him. My mates were excited about what happened. A girl my mate was talking to said, "I can see what happened - look." We all looked at the back of her dress, and there was the biggest wet stain with sand stuck to it. I puffed out my chest like a peacock. I'd had sex for the first time, and it had taken half a second. I did think there had to be more to this than what had just happened, though.

The next morning, my mates said to go down the third row of caravans. "That bird you were with on the beach is there sunbathing." They were laughing, and I sensed something fishy.

I wandered down and saw her outside the caravan with her mum. She waved, and I went over and got introduced to her mum. I could not believe it. It was there that I knew why my mates were laughing. She was a lot older than I thought. She did not have her wig on, the false eyelashes had gone, a front tooth was missing, and she had furniture disease, where her chest had dropped into her drawers.

This little head, your knob, makes you blind. If you allow it to control your life, it will destroy your dreams. You need to harness sexual power and use the same determination to achieve your goals.

I went to West Ham training, and Wally St. Pier said, "We want to sign you, Gary. Speak to your dad."

The next morning, I'm with Chelsea, and they said that they wanted me back that night, as I'm to play against Crystal Palace Youth.

Lo and behold, my dad finished work early that day and took me to the game at Hendon. That was the first time he had ever watched me play.

We got there a little late. I rushed in and got changed, and there it was, the Chelsea kit, hanging there just for me. Dad was introduced to Dave Sexton, the first team manager. That was when I realised the cut-throat business of pro football.

The way things were, I was the smallest on the pitch but also the fastest. The biggest boy on the pitch was right-back, marking me. The first time I got the ball, I went past him in a flash. Football in those days was tough. It was normal for someone to come right through the back and take your legs first and then the ball, which this fullback did to me two minutes after I flew past him. I went up in the air and landed on the back of my neck. This fullback was whispering in my ear as I got up, "You go past me again, you little cunt, and I will break your legs." You see, he was fighting for his dream as well. He did that twice more. He won the battle, and I thought, "Fuck that," and he stopped me playing. Chelsea wanted to sign me, and they reckoned they could toughen me up.

After much thought and being in a conundrum, I signed for Chelsea that night. The next day, I rang Wally St. Pier and told him I was signing for Chelsea. He wished me all the luck. He even wrote to my dad saying if it didn't work out at Chelsea, I could come back to West Ham. I stopped working with Dad, save for doing my manure round every Sunday.

Monday was my first day at Chelsea, and to my horror, on Mondays, when the first team are at home, the lads' job is to sweep the terraces. The cleaning took us the better part of the day. Then we cleaned the football boots. I was earning £15 a week with expenses. You can see why I kept doing the manure round to earn more than I did at Chelsea in one day. Regardless, it was a grounding experience.

I ask today how football is now. There are seventeen and eighteen-year-olds on £10,000 - £20,000 a week, driving a Ferrari and not even in the first team yet. Are they as hungry as we were back then? I'll leave the question open, but I will say to the Young men: You need to harness this power for everything because:

If the dream is strong enough, the facts don't count.

With football in the background, I'm still back with my girlfriend again. The hunt begins now. As the great Micky Flanagan said on stage, "The art of fingering is dead." The girls have been coached by their mums to "Keep your hand on your halfpenny," which means, don't let your knickers come down.

So, let's look at this. It takes roughly three months of hard work to eventually get your hands up her jumper. Another three months to eventually get a finger in her knickers. In those days, girls wore stockings, so when you got your hand on the lucky strip, which is between the top of the stocking and her knickers, if you get that bit of flesh, you are lucky. So, you're six months working on your dream. Then she says, "Mum and Dad are away next weekend. We can sleep together."

Bingo and long dogs, next weekend arrives, but you are holding the dream. Your girlfriend lives five miles away, and it's a Friday night. Out of nowhere, a storm hits with massive snowdrifts. You can't drive as the roads are impassable. No trains or buses are available either. Eighty-mile an hour, freezing winds are blowing, and your dream is five miles away, waiting for you. So, what do you say to yourself? "Oh well, I can't get there. Never mind."

Is that what we say? Is it fuck! We start out early and walk through ten-foot drifts and eighty-mile an hour winds. You can't see where you are going, but nothing is going to stop you from your dream. Come hell or high water, you will get there, and you do.

You girls today have a much better handle on this than the boys. You're always four years more mature than the boys. You use Nature's Power. In fact, I can see in the next twenty-five years, the world will be run by females, and there won't be any more wars.

All the young lads who have used this power for their first sexual experience, why can't they use this with everything else? Sadly, most do not, and they are like a cork in the ocean, taken by the wind and current. They have no control over where they are going, and other forces determine their future.

You may not be able to see where you are going, but nothing is going to stop you from your dream if you hold it firmly enough. Come hell or high water, you will get there.

Another big shock I experienced around this time was what adults do to children.

I made it through the snowdrifts and knocked on my girlfriend's door. She ran out with a bag packed. Her nose was bleeding, two black eyes, a split lip pouring blood and a damaged shoulder... Her dad had just beaten her up.

On the way home, she told me her dad had hit her many times before and sexually abused her. I was in so much shock hearing this. The world seemed to turn differently. How can a father do this to his daughter and a biological one at that? At the time, I didn't understand, but this determined my girlfriend's future for her life. Her subconscious mind had been hardwired. Early before, her mum had walked out of the family home and left her husband with the kids. This young girl had been sexually abused, beaten up regularly and had her mum walk out on her. Imagine that combination.

On that Friday night, she came to live with us as we had a spare bedroom. Mum agreed that she could stay at our house.

Back to football, the sport was going well. I broke into the reserve team. Chelsea had just won the FA Cup against Leeds United after a replay, and things seemed cheerful. There were times I was training with the first team, and it felt great.

But then, bang - my first big mistake at the club. When I look back at the situation, I was being sent the right way, but I didn't know it at the time. All mistakes are given to us for learning. You never fail - you learn.

A good friend of mine asked if I would play in a Cup semi-final the following Sunday. I said, "Alfie, I can't, mate. I'm not allowed to as I have a contract." He pestered me, and he said that nobody would know. I ended up playing and tore this opposite team apart in the first half. The second half - bang. I was out for eight weeks with a fractured shinbone.

When I went on Monday to Chelsea, they suspended me for eight weeks and said when I came back, I'd be back with the juniors. My contract was torn up.

The football dream was shattered, but now I understood I'd taken the focus off the dream, and other things had taken over. That was another lesson that you must hold onto the dream picture until it's complete. I probably thought I'd made it and let the dream go too early.

On that Monday morning, I started working with Dad and learned plastering and building, which in the future came in handy. I got myself a little van, and away we went. My girlfriend and I were the same as normal - together, not together -

but it was hard because she lived at my house. Her jealousy was getting worse, but in those days, I didn't understand. We could be walking through the High Street, and she would see a girl on the other side of the road, and before I'd even noticed, she would say, "Look at her, and you're dead." This happened when we went out as well. It got so bad I would never talk to any females. It's only in the past twenty years that I have lost that feeling.

We decided to get married, and I had my stag do on a Friday night. We had a great laugh down at the Brighton Run, which was only up the road. Me and Stan, my best man, were waiting in the church as my now-to-be-wife walked up the aisle. She got alongside me, and I said she looked beautiful. She looked at me and said in a loud voice, "After the ceremony, we are divorcing. You were with girls last night."

Joke
Marriage is like a grenade. Pull the ring, and you lose your house.

Your Notes

Chapter 5: New Directions

Failures are a bridge, not a wall.

We lived in a caravan at the bottom of the garden near the stables. I was learning plastering and building, but deep down, I knew I would not do this for the rest of my life. I believed something would come my way one day.

On a lovely sunny afternoon, we were rendering a building three floors up on a scaffold. On the third storey scaffold, there were now three of us plasterers, Dad, Dick, and me. Pete, the labourer, was on the ground, loading up the board and easel with sand and cement. Dad was at one end of the scaffold board, and Dick was at the other. I was waiting at the top of the ladder for Pete to climb up and deliver the next load of muck. Health & Safety were non-existent in those days.

Dad and Dick both walked to the centre of the scaffold board at the same time. There was a click, the puck links came out of the wall, and down we went. It was the summer, and I was in my shorts with no top on. I learned that day that you go down quicker than coming up. I came down and landed on the bottom rung with each leg on either side of a pole, with the board and easel, sand and cement, all on top of me. Don't worry, the pole missed my nuts, and thankfully so.

I looked at my dad, and he was hanging upside down with his leg through a fanlight window. Dick went straight to the ground and was knocked out. People came running out, and they helped Dad down. Then it was my turn. Finally, Dick woke up too. A piece of four-by-two with six-inch nails sticking out of it had missed his hand by inches.

He woke up, looked at the four-by-two and passed out again. While this was happening, Pete, who had stayed on the ground, was rushing to ring for an ambulance. When he walked into a metal up-and-over garage door, it split his head wide open. The ambulance turned up, and Pete, the labourer, who was on the ground when the scaffold collapsed, was the only one who went to the hospital. All we lost was skin, but we got an education free of cost.

Apart from that, work was going well. Home life was turning to rat shit, though. I was getting just as bad as my wife. I was no angel, and we were both fighting like dogs and cats.

Dad taught me how to plaster ceilings. I could plaster walls, but not ceilings. The tricky part with plastering ceilings is, you have to keep your head out of the way. We had a plaster called Thistle, which went on boards, and you added lime in to make it a smoother mix. First trowelful and a big blob of plaster went straight into my eye. Fuck me, the pain was excruciating. The lime was burning my eye. Dad grabbed the hosepipe and washed it out. It took three days for my eye to open until I could see out of it. Another lesson learned, and that never happened again.

All of this was teaching me that there is a difference between wisdom and experience. Wisdom is when you listen to your elders and apply their advice. Experience is when you ignore advice and carry on to get the experience.

Then we had a crisis. I woke up one morning and couldn't move. My back was killing me, and I had pain down my leg. When Dad came home from work, we went to the hospital. I had a bad back and needed bed rest. Got physiotherapy for weeks, but I was no better. The physio said, "We can't do anything for you, and you're to wear a corset." I said I was going on holiday with my wife and friends. This completely fucks up the street cred and the suntan.

You see, all this happened *for* me, not *to* me: to change my direction in life. Things that I thought were falling apart were coming together.

One of Dad's friends said, "Send him to an osteopath." I went, and in six weeks, this man put me right. He said this had happened due to a heavy fall - the scaffold collapsing. While I was in the waiting room, there was a fantastic, great-looking girl there. Her name was called, and she went in. I thought, "Wow, she is going to go in there, take her clothes off and pay the osteopath to look at her." When you're young like I was, I thought I would love that job. At my last appointment, I was asking him all sorts of questions. He could see my interest and gave me the name of a college to find out more.

The next day I said to Dad, "I'm going to be an osteopath." He looked at me and said, "You stupid cunt. You have no chance, as long as you have a hole in your arse." My dad was a hardworking man who made his family secure, but he was not the most positive person. I stood there thinking, "Fuck you, I am. I'm doing it. Just to prove you wrong." I often wonder, did he say that just to make me move and inspire me, or was he just actually negative?

As I had no qualifications, no A-Levels, I couldn't go to the British School of Osteopathy without a grant, but there was a northern school that I could attend and pay for. Dad said he was not going to pay for that. He said, for one, I would pack up halfway through, and secondly, if I paid, I would probably manage to do it.

My books arrived, and I started to study. I was working with Dad and studying even while I was at work. We would have lunch and tea breaks. Everyone got their newspapers out, and I got my Anatomy & Physiotherapy book out. They really took the piss.

You see, when you start something different, Nature wants to know if you really want it or not. It will give you a hard time. Nature knows, if you come through it, you will win. And remember, you win or learn, you never lose.

I would work with Dad, save my money, go away to Blackpool to do practical work, come back with more books, and learn the theory. I had a new dream, which was asserting that:

When the dream is big enough, the facts don't count.

The wife and I were at war, mostly when I went away. Most times, I took her with me. So, as many young couples do when they are not getting along, we also said, "Let's have a baby. That will make things better."

I was lucky with my upbringing and school. Remember, I said that Nature's Power gives us clues when we are young. Around this time that I was studying every night, I laid in bed going through my own little movie with my eyes shut, watching clients come into my Clinic, waiting in Reception and going into my treatment room. I visualised this every day until that happened… and it did.

I started to build an extension on the side of Mum and Dad's house for the wife and me to live in and for my Clinic. We lived there for a short time, not getting on any better. The wife was pregnant with our first child. We moved into our first little house, hoping this would change things for the better.

I passed the first course, which was a remedial massage, and started to get clients. We had our first child, a little girl, and things changed for a while. The wife was totally in love with our daughter, and she was at peace. The clinic was growing nicely as I had pictured, and money was rolling in. Things were looking up between us.

Then bang, as it occurs with life, it all started again, and I began playing football with my mates. I was busy at the clinic, so I was not the perfect husband, and Dad and I were getting accused of everything. I am taking all this stick, fuck it. I had an affair, which made me happy for half an hour, but it was not the right thing to do.

Little head controlling the big head again.

While this was going on, my wife fell pregnant again. I left the house for a while but was at the birth of our second child. I moved back in, and we moved to Tillingham. I had two beautiful daughters in a new house, a new location and a new life. I was getting really busy in the clinic in Wickford. I bought a villa in Spain. The kids were at school, and it was going great.

Then it kicked off again. I was just as much to blame, but I will admit that people are selfish.

One day I had a lady in my clinic whom I had never seen before. She said, "Gary, I haven't met you before. You have an aura around you, and with you is an Egyptian who is your guardian." I was dumbfounded, but it makes sense now. How did she know that?

When my wife and I got back together again, we went to Egypt. When I stood at the bottom of the Great Pyramid, I felt I had been there before, which goes back to my first junior school days. I had made a miniature pyramid with the slaves made out of pipe cleaners pulling a large stone.

I now believe that when the body dies, the spirit lives on and that infinite intelligence is available for all of us to use. How much wisdom is there?

Just believe in Nature's power.

This lady left my clinic, and I never saw her again, but before she left, she said to me, "Sometimes you have to change partners. I think it is time for you to do that." How did she know that too? What a mysterious clairvoyant.

That was when I decided to draw a line in the sand and never cross it again. I left the next day. I could not put my girls through the war again.

Joke

Mother-in-law said to me the other day, "My joints are stiff."

I said, "You're rolling them too tight."

Your Notes

Chapter 6: The Start of an Incredible Journey

If you are at the end of your rope, tie a knot at the end and hang in there.

I am not going into the finer details, but my divorce happened, and it took five years. I didn't see my girls for three years. I believed I was taking divorce for my girls but was I?

I was back to living at the clinic with my head in turmoil—all negative thoughts. And to top it all off, I lurched straight into another relationship. We rented a house in Woodham because I'd left the previous house to my wife. I would rather live in a tent and be happy.

Then the strangest thing happened. A man who was a client of mine left a package for me to go through that night with my partner. This was to be the start of an incredible journey, which created my long-lasting dream and the reason why I'm writing this, to help as many people as I can. I want to change your thinking and to give you hope, the likes of which I received.

I want to let you know about Nature's Power. It's for everyone to use in a positive way. The book we read that night and the tape we listened to sold us on the dream. I didn't know what it was about it, but we were now excited about the future.

I told this man we were interested. He said, "I will come down to your house in two days' time, but while I'm showing you the secret, invite some friends round, and we will show them at the same time."

We did as he suggested. I had about ten people in the room, and he showed us the Amway business. The next night, we went to our first meeting in Hatfield. It was mind-blowing, and we got hooked on the dream. The man who had told us about Amway said to me, "One day, Gary, you will be up there on that platform, speaking."

I thought, "No way. I can't lead in silent prayer. I'm shy. No way."

We went to Wembley and saw a bigger picture. We have now taken the bait, hook, line and sinker. Then our life changed. For the first time, I was reading motivational and self-help books. I didn't know it at the time, but this was me chasing my biggest dream ever.

For the next twenty-five years, I have found myself on an incredible journey that has been given to me so that I can help others lead a happy life.

If you are happy, you are healthy.

As I have said earlier, as a child, Nature's Power gives us clues. We grow up and learn all about the strangest secret. But to those of you who haven't, be open and ready.

Let the journey begin.

***

The biggest criminals of today are those of us with eyes but who refuse to read.

I'm into my second marriage by now, and we managed to get a mortgage and bought a little house in South Woodham. I have the clinic in Wickford and now the Amway business.

If there are some young people reading this, I do recommend you to join a good networking group in your spare time. It is an incredible way of learning about people, life and struggles, failures, and hard work. You will mix with very positive people, have encouraging meetings and read helpful books. You will be set for life.

Our group, we started out on the road. I had to do my first meeting in a house. I had never spoken in front of anybody, let alone speak about a business which I didn't fully understand, but as I have been saying:

If the dream is strong enough, the facts don't count.

When I got to the first meeting. I was shitting myself, but I'm reading every day, listening to tapes every day: *face the fear, and it will run away.* I walked in and set up my whiteboard, hands shaking, and I'm well out of my comfort zone. I was preparing what to do and how to introduce myself.

See, when you start these meetings, you are helping people to start a business and teach them at the same time. It's an anxious business for a novice. I was sweating, and ten people were joining. I was going over my presentation, and guess what happens? Nobody turns up.

I was relieved but then gutted too because I've still got to go through my first one again.

You learn about promotional events, books and audiotapes. In those days, you had to get good at promotions, but you had to get the people to plug into a system. They need this in the early days. If you don't get them going to a monthly meeting, they refuse to read. They will never build this type of business. I will cover all this in later chapters, especially the Crab Basket.

So another meeting is arranged, and one person turns up. I start. The man jumps and says, "Is this Amway?" I tell him it is. He says, "Don't want to know," and leaves. The couple I was doing the meeting for quit that night.

After three weeks of doing meetings with people who attended, all of them quit. Do you think I was having doubts? I was. I doubted myself. Could I do this? I would ask. But then I went to another meeting and bang - I was ready to go again.

Monday night, I'm off to Ruislip in London. Sunday night, we had an Indian meal, and when I'm nervous, my stomach goes, and I must get to the toilet quickly. The traffic was heavy, but I got there on time. I ran in and said to the host, "Set the board up, I must use your toilet." He said, "Gary, the toilet is here," which was just off the lounge where the meeting was being held.

As I rushed to the toilet, I knew there were people in the room just on the other side of the wall. I sat on the toilet, and I could easily hear their voices. Horror and panic - if I can hear them, they will definitely hear me.

I'm trying to let this gas from the Indian out quietly. The more you pucker, the louder the noise. I probably cut off the biggest fart of my life so far. I discovered you can't cough and fart at the same time. You cough to cover up the noise, cough and the fart comes straight after.

I turned the taps on, trying to cover the noise that is coming out of my arse. I couldn't hear the people talking as they were busy listening. I finished, composed myself and walked out and pretended nothing had happened.

I went up to the board, and a man said, "I hope this business is not a load of shit like you just did in there." It broke the ice, and everyone laughed. Three people got into the business that night. Funny how things happen, eh?

When you set up this type of business and have meetings, you can't have animals or children running around. You want the focus on the board.

I had a meeting in Pitsea on a hot summer night. It was really hot. This couple had two Rottweilers, big dogs. They had them shut in the kitchen. I'm halfway through when these dogs walked in, and the room went quiet. I stopped talking, and they walked around the room, looked at everyone and were walking back into the kitchen when one of them farted. He must have been eating cabbage for a fortnight; the stink was horrendous. People climbed out of the windows, two big blokes, they rushed for the door and got stuck. It was fucking mayhem.

That was the end of that meeting, and the couple quit.

There were so many occasions that were so funny and life-changing. I was very quickly learning about people. I could write a complete book on meetings, but I think you're getting the idea.

The one thing that is fishy with networking is, they tell you that you can become financially independent, and it's true, you can. But they never tell you that it's hard work every day, going through the numbers. Any success in any business and life comes from sheer hard work. Nobody just steps into success.

We went to a weekend meeting where I met for the very first time, a man called Bill O'Brian. This man changed my life and thinking, and so did another man, Fred Hartis.

The business started to roll. I was driving all over the country. I was listening to tapes on the road. I was putting on the Rocky theme just before I got to the meetings, so I was wired and fired up as I walked in. This networking business teaches you about yourself.

My second wife and I were involved with this. She was becoming very positive, and now she wanted a child. She had never been married before and had no children. Here was another girl who had been mentally and physically abused. I do attract these women, I thought, or are there just too many out there? I believe there are, and some carry this to their graves.

As you know, I have two daughters from my first marriage. I had a vasectomy, and I walked out of the doctors that day, having just had the operation, and I said to myself, "I'm going to have a son."

I said to my second wife, "Are you sure you can have children?" and she replied, "I don't see why not." We set up the plan for me to have a reversal, which is a slightly bigger operation. The specialist said there was only a 50% chance this would work.

On the day of the operation, I had to shave off my pubic hair, much to the amusement of the wife. I looked down, and it looked like a plucked chicken.

I had the operation, and when I woke, there was a scaffolding of sticky tape all around my parts. They were huge and painful, but you go through this for the dream - which, at the time, was my son. After ten days, I had to pull off the sticky strapping and let the air get to the wound. I'm in the bath soaking. Nobody ever had told me to shave my arse; the sticky tape is nicely stuck to the hair. I slowly and painfully pull each bit out, and the wife is knocking outside asking if she can help, amongst the giggles. I said she could help by fucking off and leaving me to it.

Eventually, it's all off, and I have the biggest pair of blue balls I have ever seen. After a few weeks, I had to take my semen in a jar and keep it warm for tests. I had a low count, but we had live ones.

My first divorce was over, and my ex-wife got the house. My two girls had regular payments made every week. The day after it had all been settled, I received a call from the Inland Revenue, saying they understood I had a villa in Spain, which I'd paid cash for. They wanted to see me in their offices the next day.

I was in their office with my accountant, and he was great. He said he had done Mr Price's books with the information that was provided and left. I asked the Inspector who had told him about the villa, and he said he couldn't tell me. I said, "Was it my ex-wife?" and he just smiled.

The questions started. He said, "We have worked out what we think you owe, and it's £900,000."

I said, "You're joking me." He said, "No, sir. Can you prove that you don't owe this figure?"

I had to go back every month for a year, but I was reading all sorts of things about building a positive mental attitude. They were not going to take my mind - I would come out the other side. I saw three Inspectors, and they couldn't get the better of my mind.

In the end, I was beginning to enjoy the battles. The last Inspector said, "This has been going on for too long, Mr Price, and we needed to settle this."

I said, "Well, you gave me a silly figure, and I can't prove I have not earned that, and you can't prove I have. Let's be sensible and have a feasible figure." We agreed on £35,000. I sold the villa and paid the Inland Revenue.

I still had the clinic, and the network business was growing. We are trying for a baby, but nothing is happening. My wife went to the doctor to have tests. There was something inside her womb which was killing the sperm before they started on their journey.

Great, I thought. I go through all the reversal and pain, and she is killing my sperm. The doctor gave her this trumpet looking thing with a big puffer on the end to put inside her and pump a solution inside. Then we were to have sex straight away.

The doctor said what he could do was to send us to a specialist in this field, but we could only do it three times. We went to the specialist, and he explained they had to inject my wife every day when she was producing eggs, and when they moved down into position, they could take the sperm and inject them into the womb. He said he was just a taxi driver. I injected my wife with the solution every day, and when she was ovulating, I put the sperm into the jar. She then drove off to the specialist, keeping it warm. We did this twice, and it didn't work.

When we had started the networking business, a speaker had said to me that you should write down in detail what you want in life and how your life is going to be. Read this every night. Don't miss a night and if you do, start again. Do this for twelve months, and in the future, you will have everything you asked for.

The first thing on my list was a son. This was fermented in my subconscious, so I knew it will happen. I had to be all about belief and faith.

We started again. On a Friday night, I went to my mate's birthday bash. The day before, I put my back out.

Saturday morning, the wife went to the specialist for X-rays to see if the eggs were ready. They were. She rang and said I had to get there as fast as I could and do a sample there. I'm hungover, and I've got a bad back, I'm walking like I have something stuck sideways, and I've got to drive to Chelmsford and pop into a newsagent to buy a girlie mag.

I arrived at the hospital, a nurse was waiting for me. She led me to a waiting room toilet and told me to go in and give her the jar as soon as I could. Now, if you could imagine my plight. A waiting room toilet with lots of patients outside.

I went into the toilet, which was small, I might add, and I thumbed through the magazine. Propped that on the radiator, and my back is killing me. With the knob in one hand and the jar in the other, we start. I'm struggling, but I press on as I want a boy. Things start to liven up, and then there's a knock on the door. A man says, "Will you be long?" and bang - the knob drops like a stone, the magazine falls on the floor, and I drop the jar.

I was struggling with my back to pick up the mag and the jar and started again. I have my wife in a room on the bed with her legs in the air waiting for me. I had lost momentum, but I crack on.

I just got to the vinegar strokes when the nurse knocks on the door, saying, "Please hurry up, Mr Price." The knob drops like a stone once again, and I say to her, "If you would like to come in here, we can get the job done." She laughs and says, "Hurry up," and walks off.

At last, the job was done, and I walked out into the waiting room with the people smiling at me as they all knew what I had been doing. I thought, Fuck it, I want a son. The nurse ran off with the jar, and I sat down and waited.

The specialist came out and said, "I have injected seventy million sperm into your wife, and there are three ripe eggs. Let's see." I had never banged one out in the toilet before, and I don't want that ever again. But think, seventy million sperm and that was low. Everyone on the planet is the best, the strongest and the fastest because they won the race against seventy million sperm.

Bingo, it worked. The wife is pregnant, and we are moving to a house in Wickford. The clinic is going well. Network business is booming, and we hit a high level. I'm invited to speak at Wembley and tell our story.

This was a defining moment, to walk out at Wembley to four thousand people. My hands were shaking, trying to hold it together. This business had got me this far. A shy lad, smallest in the class, biggest ears, who on occasions still stuttered. After five minutes, I calmed down and started to walk up and down. While on the stage, I found out that I had a talent for making people laugh.

We got a standing ovation.

I was out every night, building the network business and speaking around the country at weekends. It was growing fast, really fast, because of the system we had. We were filling arenas, NIA, NEC, G Max Manchester, all in the same weekend. It's not until you reach a higher level that you get money from the system.

Months later, it turns out that we had a baby boy, just as I had visualised. We moved to a bigger house in Wickford, and we were on our way up. We started to see the girls again in that my eldest moved in. Two years later, my youngest moved in as well. My mum and dad were over the moon because they were seeing their granddaughters again and a new grandson.

My close Auntie and Uncle, Kit and Bill, they passed away around this time. They left me their bungalow, which I sold, and put deposits on four small houses, with "buy to let" mortgages, to rent out. We were going flat-out, running the clinic and out every night building the network business. Now, we had four houses to look after.

Suddenly, there was a downturn in the business, unrest with some of the leaders. The business system became massive, and we were earning more from building the system than from Amway. The top leaders in America were earning millions, and so were the top earners in this country. The meeting attendances were dropping in size so much that we could only half fill the NEC. The groups were getting much smaller, and then I met a man called Dave Bevan. I was impressed with him, so I took half of my group and joined Herbalife.

Months later, Amway pulled the plug on all systems. It collapsed, and I had seen this coming. That's why I moved. The stress of that and moving companies, with all my time spent on the road and leaving my wife to handle a new home and a baby, cracks started to appear. I never realised at the time, but my wife's past was returning to haunt her. Those dark files were coming to the front again.

She was frequenting a hypnotherapist. The woman wanted to know what happened and by whom.

The next three months were horrendous. I'm not putting all the details down, but this smashed a close family apart. It was very difficult to keep positive. I stopped reading, and I was in that rut of despair and confusion; basically, everything was a mess. The Amway business was collapsing, my hard work was disappearing, my wife was in a very dark place, and my absence had not really helped.

I thought I would help the situation by shagging the sister in law. I kept that quiet and hidden for a time. This wasn't one of my better moves, in fact, I completely destroyed everything. This gave me the lesson:

You are where you are today because of decisions you made in the past. Cause and effect. What you do always comes back to you.

We sold the four houses, sold the house in Wickford and bought a house in Hanningfield. A new start. We achieved the "Millionaire Team" in the Herbalife business in a year, and I still had the clinic.

I unpacked my stuff in the new office and found my old Filofax, and opened it. I pulled out a piece of paper, and it was my dream page, which I mentioned earlier, my life, how I wanted it to be. I had read this every night for a year, but I had not looked at it in four years.

I sat there in the office and started to read it again. First, I'd wanted a son, then a detached house with an acre of land, a football pitch, a big pond, an S-type Mercedes, a 4x4 and two Boxer dogs.

I was reading this in my office, which was halfway down the garden and was left sitting there in amazement because everything I'd written down was here with me. This meant I needed new dreams and to return to the system.

Things started to settle down, and I was back to speaking every weekend and going abroad. But my wife wasn't the same person. I had a secret.

I would like to say now to any husband who is, or has been, cheating on their wife, if you think you have got away with it, you are wrong, your wife knows.

Remember, the great Fred Hartis said:

The truth sets you free.

I had fallen out of love with my wife on her decision to find out her past, and she fell out of love with me because I was not the same man. I thought we could start over again if I told her what I had done, and we could get over it.

But how wrong was I. Bang - the family was at war. All because of a wrong decision I had made in the past.

We struggled for a year, living in the same house, and I was back and forth, away every weekend, speaking. We were staying together for the wrong reason - my son. One day, as I had in the past, I drew a line in the sand. Here was another marriage gone.

We sold the dream house and bought a house outright with the proceeds. I'm back at the clinic at Mum and Dad's house. My daughter had already left. The eldest had moved to London, nearer to where my youngest daughter had moved in with her mate. I had to make a decision. Do I keep speaking every weekend, earn lots of money, or do I spend that time with my son?

I quit Herbalife for more time with my son. Memories are far more important to him than money. Thankfully, there were no restrictions on when I saw him. If you spoke to him today, you would never know he came from a broken home, unlike my daughters, unfortunately.

Remember when I said I was in my new office reading out my dream goals sheet, and I had achieved everything on that sheet? My biggest mistake was I hadn't written another one. I thought I had arrived. But the truth is, you need to always keep setting the dream and goals and keep chasing.

Nature's Power - stop using it and you'll lose it.

The brain is like a fruit. When a fruit is ripe, but it's not put to use, it goes rotten. Keep the brain and the mind green. Never stop learning.

When you are plugged into a positive reading programme, if you stop, you turn off the power. Like a fan, it loses the power in its spin, then it eventually stops. I stopped reading, so I was like a cork on the ocean, bobbing around and letting the waves carry me. The only direction I had was my son, and we were together every week.

The relationship I had with my dad went sour because he blamed me for my broken marriages and giving all the money to my second wife.

I was on a downward spiral. I had read over two hundred books, which had taken me to where I was, and then I stopped reading. Now life was riding me, not the other way around.

And like the previous time, there I am in another relationship with a lady who had two children. It was doomed from the start, but we still got married. We bought a little bungalow, and I turned it into a five-bedroom house, which I had built myself. While we were doing that, the marriage kept going. When we had finished, the cracks started to appear.

We had nothing in common. I used to dread going home, and probably she dreaded me coming home.

I was back to my books, and one day I read: "When there is no love at the table, it is time to leave."

During this downward period, my mum had died. In other words, my world, my inspiration, my fun, had died. I was drinking too much and was always angry. From a man who had reached the top, I was back down to rock bottom. My dad was ill and was on his way down in life. He couldn't cope without Mum.

I drew a line in the sand again, left the wife in the home I had just built, and moved back to the clinic to look after Dad.

Another marriage ended, and another home lost.

It was then, on New Year's Eve, that my life changed again, for good, permanently. I hadn't known it at the time, but that's the night I met my soulmate, Julie.

My dad had two strokes, and it was a good thing I had moved back. After several weeks, Julie moved in to help too. My youngest daughter had moved in with her boyfriend, so we were all there for Dad. All of us being in the same house was hard at times, but we all pulled together. Julie and I were developing a special bond, which I had never known were possible before. She was helping me, and I was helping her. I was back on track reading.

This was a testament to the fact that you can lose it all, but you can get it back by using Nature's Power the right way.

I took Julie to see Tony Robbins, the nation's top life and business strategist. It was my second time seeing him. We walked the hot coals together. That night changed Julie forever. Spending four days listening to Tony started a chain of positive thoughts and dreams. You see, Julie was one of those mentally and physically abused children who had missed out on Nature's Power as a child. Now, after seeing Tony Robbins, she started to do what she had always wanted, to write her book, her story, Out of the Frying Pan and Into the Fire.

Now we were on a new journey together for the rest of our lives.

***

Our first dream together was to own our own restaurant, which we did for six months. Julie ran it, and I cooked, as that was my favourite pastime. It lasted six months. Managing it was hard but fun, and we loved being together. I was still running the clinic, looking after Dad and running a restaurant; one of the two had to go - the restaurant.

Julie used to cut my dad's toenails and massage his feet. I used to say to her, "How on earth can you do that?" and she said, "I don't mind feet." I said to Julie, "You need to go and learn to become a foot health professional and work in the clinic," and so she did.

She became a foot health professional, and I'm so proud of her. From where she started to where she is today is a miracle. She is the most caring person I have ever known, and now she has her own private healthcare company, and I'm her hero. We are now a great team, on a journey together, using Nature's Power to the fullest. What we had pictured has come to pass.

When Dad passed away, we wrote down the next chapter for the house and the garden and planned to get married in the garden which I had grown up in. We pictured this for two years. We worked on the house, and on 25th August 2018, we got married in the garden. All that we had pictured was there.

Now we are on our journey to help as many people as possible. Me, I am now complete. I have a wife who completes me.

This is my story so far. The learning part of life, and I'm still learning. Now it's time for me to give back and go for my biggest dream.

I have been giving you hints of what Nature's Power or God is, whichever phrase you want to use. Some of you have got it, but most people have not.

In the next section, those of you who have not will get it.

Joke

A lady in a supermarket says, "Hi there."

The man in the supermarket replies, "Do I know you?"

Lady says, "I think you are the father of one of my kids."

Man says, "Oh no. Are you the stripper I made love to on a pool table last year while my mates were watching, and your partner was hitting my bum with a celery stick?"

Lady says: "No… I am your son's schoolteacher."

Your Notes

Chapter 7: The Training

All power comes from within, so it is within your control.

We begin on a long journey, understanding Nature's Power, which we all use every day either *against* us or *for* us. It's your choice.

As Earl Nightingale said in 'The Strangest Secret', "Men today just do not think. What we think about all day long is what we will become." As a young man, when I first read that, it worried me. I thought, shit, I think about girls most of the time, so I will wake up one morning as a girl. That could come in handy for 24 hours max, perhaps… but I like being a male. Sorry - it's just my humour.

In the last thirty years, I have read hundreds of books and still read today. I spend every day with people of wisdom who are teaching me: people who are long gone, whose wisdom is preserved in the written word. I have spent time with people who are no longer here, as well as with the living legends of today. You keep the mind green and never stop learning.

My belief, and that of many, is that the body dies, but the spirit lives on. The intelligence is up there. Infinite intelligence is available to everyone. You just have to believe.

Let's think of it this way. How many times have you thought of someone you have not seen for a while, and the next day, you see them, or they call you? What is *déjà vu*?

Wherever you are now, stop reading and look around. Are you at home, in an arena, a stadium, a car or at work? Every single thing you see around you right now was, at one time, just a thought. A thought that was in someone's mind only, and yet with willpower, passion and repetition of that thought, the reality materialised.

You need the dream and the willpower to keep repeating to your subconscious mind the dream vision, like the Kango hammer: knock, knock, knock, until it breaks. With today's technology that's advancing at a rapid pace, mobile phones and iPads, laptops, watches that talk to you and pay your bills with an app, CTC, you can maximise this repetition habit through resources such as calendar, alarms, etc. These devices were all just a thought some years ago.

Without thought, we would still be running around the jungle.

Apply the analogy of the computer to yourself. Your tongue is your mouse. You are hung by your tongue. What you put into the computer comes out. It's a testament that:

Nature: if you plant nettles, you do not get roses.

If you get banged up in prison for twenty years, you don't come out a copper. If you put seeds or a plant into the ground and you water and tend to them, they flourish. You plant a seed and bury it in the soil, water it every day and believe that in a week, you will see a shoot. You don't simply after one day say, "That ain't working," and dig out the plant.

No, you believe.

It's the same with a thought. Keep repeating and believing, and it will materialise. Don't say, "I tried for a day, and it doesn't work." Make your thoughts your compost heap. Give them time while also tending to them.

When you have your first child, and they are trying to walk for the first time, they will try, wobble, and they will fall. You, as a parent, don't say, "Right, that's it, you will never walk, so don't try it again." No, you encourage them to do the opposite: keep trying, and it will happen.

Similarly, most people FAIL their way to success. Failure doesn't mean stopping: failure means learning.

Dreams are set in cement. Plans to achieve the dream are set in sand. If one way fails, Nature's Power will find another way, which, when you look back, would actually turn out to be the easiest route.

Nothing on this Earth can stop a human being who has will, passion and holds a positive picture in front of them. For as long as it takes, it will happen.

The subconscious mind is powerful, but it does not know the difference between truth and fiction: it acts upon the picture that is hammered into it. The subconscious mind can cure or cause any condition. It depends on what information it has been given.

So, success can be perceived differently, in different forms:
- A woman who wants to be a great mother
- A man or woman who wants a better job, a bigger house, a better car
- Someone who wants to run their own business
- A holiday home
- To travel more
- Getting a pair of shoes, which at the moment they can't afford
- The right partner to marry
- It's endless

The great Gary Vaynerchuk said recently, "One of the biggest diseases in society today is regret." Think about that. Was there any time an opportunity came your way, and you never jumped at the chance? It could be a girl of your dreams who you never had the courage to speak to? In such moments, you were using Nature's Power *against* you.

Every young person has been given a gift. Every young male and female has dreams and goals of where they want to be in life, but what the fuck happens? Unknowingly, they use Nature's Power *against* themselves.

There are people in this world who just march towards success in their lives, not knowing about Nature's Power, but using it subconsciously all the time. They just think it is natural to think "success", but they are wrong. Their gift was given to them by Nature.

There are artists who had been given gifts and became world stars but had negative thoughts which destroyed them:

Whitney Houston, Amy Whitehouse, Michael Jackson, Elvis Presley, Robin Williams, George Best, Paul (Gazza) Gascoigne, to name just a few.

I have known people, and all they wanted was money. They got lots of it. All the toys you could imagine - millionaires. They are not happy people; they profess that money is the root of all evil. That is actually untrue… the LOVE of money is evil. Some people just want power.

Everyone wants to be happy. If you are happy inside, you are happy outside. Happiness first, then your health and money will turn up naturally. Find your happiness and then the dream before yearning to earn money and health.

There is probably a man somewhere in a far-removed place in a hut, living off the land, fishing and earning less than £10,000 a year because that has always been his dream. He is a wealthy man because that is what he always wanted. Happiness.

Happiness, health, money - always in that order. Remove anger, hatred, regret and fear from your mind, and you will be healthy. You can eat at the table of abundance. The more you give, the more you receive. Give someone a smile, and you get a smile back in some other form, from another source. Give someone a compliment, and you will make their day. This is Nature - what you give out, you get back. Cast your bread across the water, and it comes back buttered. Hold a positive picture long enough in your mind, and it will materialise.

Joke

Wife in the kitchen making breakfast, and the husband walks in to see his wife in a tiny T-shirt. Wife turns around looks at him and said. "I need you now." She lays on the kitchen table with the T-shirt up around her neck.

The husband, in his surprise leaps on. When he is done, he stands up and says, "What was that all about?"

Wife says, "The egg timer has broken."

Your Notes

Chapter 8: Dreams and Will

Pay now or pay later, but you will pay. Later is more expensive.

Let me tell you a story of a dream with a will to succeed.

Remember when I said my dad had horses? Well, six in total and all kept in stables. The first of the six was Survival, the stallion, which was used for stud, kept in stable No. 1. In stable No. 6 was Country Girl, and that was Survival's dream girl. He used to look out of his stable, just watching her. He would ignore the other mares. Every time we took Country Girl out, he would go berserk.

This was his dream, Survival's dream. He wanted Country Girl, and he wanted her badly.

One day Dad said, "Right. Country Girl is in season, and we will mate her." I took Country Girl out of the stable and around the back to the other side of the farm gate. Dad put on the white bridle, and Survival was ready. I pushed Country Girl back up at the gate. Dad and the stallion came roaring around the other side.

Survival, in fact, had five legs. He was snorting, his eyes were bulging, and he could see his dream. If you think this is fantasy, trust me, I would not make this up. Country Girl's minge was winking, and she was ready. I pulled her forward, and the stallion was pulling my dad with him.

Survival got on two legs and jumped on. My job was to hold Country Girl with one hand and pull the stallion's foreleg up and hold it. Dad's job was to hold the stallion with one hand and, with the other, direct Survival's huge knob into the right direction.

The problem with this arrangement was that Country Girl was over 17 hands, and Survival was 16 hands. Because this was his dream, he naturally got too excited and rushed on… but since he was too low, he shot a bucket-load of semen all over my legs.

Dad had a plan. He took Survival back to the stable, and I took Country Girl back to hers. He said to leave the horses in for an hour and went for a cup of tea. Dick and me were to dig a big hole on Dad's command. He took us round the back of the stables and showed us what he wanted, how wide and how deep. So, we dug the hole. The theory was that if Country Girl's back legs are in the hole, she will be the right height for Survival.

So, here we go again. Same procedure. I back up Country Girl to the gate, and she is ready, but this time I have the help of Dick on the other side to hold and pull Survival on. Dad came around with Survival, the stallion's eyes bulging. He was not going to miss this time. Country Girl's back legs were in the hole. Survival jumped on. Dad, who had hands like digger buckets, grabbed Survival's knob.

To tell you how big this thing was, my dad's finger and thumb did not meet. You can let your imagination run.

With this assistance, Survival gave a massive push so hard that he pushed Country Girl out of the hole. This was his dream, and he was having it. We held his legs. The horse grabbed Dick's curly hair between his teeth to hang on. I looked underneath Country Girl, and I could see Survival's back legs dangling in the wind. I couldn't stop laughing.

My dad was shouting, "Stop fucking laughing and hold on!" Dick was shouting, "The fucking horse has got my hair!" and I'm laughing uncontrollably at this chaotic scene. I looked into Survival's eyes. I can't emphasize enough that this was his dream - I could tell just by his body language - and he was having it, no matter what. Then there's a massive fart from Survival, and he's finished. And it is here that the idea that had been brewing subconsciously fermented some more:

When the dream is big enough the facts do not count.

That was nature at its most natural, seeking a little help and push from humans.

Can you see the theme developing? A dream or goal, persistence, will, belief. These are the combinations that matter in life!

Let me tell you about a young man who went to university and came out with a degree in illustrating and drawing cartoon characters. He had a gift, but a change was occurring, and technology was here. Computers had made it into this world and were becoming the next big thing. This man got a job with a company that was doing graphics on TV shows. He was the gofer all around Soho and the tea boy as well.

He went to another company in the same field, and once again, he was the gofer; go for this and go for that. In his spare time after work and at weekends, he would watch others and learn computers and computer programming. The dream was there but also caught in the net of change.

Remember: whether your dreams are in cement or plans in the sand, just believe with full force that it will happen, and nature will lead you the right way.

The man went to another small company that was doing the same things, learning computer programming and graphics in his spare time as well as being the tea boy.

How many graduates would have given up by now already? The dream in this young man was so big that come hell or high water, he was not going to back down. He then moved on to another larger company and again learned what he could in his spare time. Do you think he would question himself sometimes? Was it easy for him keeping that dream alive? To bring the attention to the quote again:

Dream big enough and the facts do not count.

As it turned out, he had a positive uncle who said to him one day: "If you ever get the opportunity to grasp your dream job, but you feel you are not ready, always say 'Yes' and nature will guide you." Thankfully, this young man could now be more bent on what he could achieve than what was immediately before him.

One day that opportunity came through finally. The manager said, "Can you do that?" and the young man said, "Yes."

Was it easy for him? No. There were ups and downs, and the question was running within himself, too: Can I do this? But you see, when you have the dream in front of you, nature wants to see if you are serious. Hence, he replied yes. So, ask yourself, is your dream big enough or are you merely giving it lip service? The hardest wood in the world is the Canadian Redwood. Know why? Because they grow in the strongest of winds so that harsh survival makes them strong.

The young man learned his trade doing graphics on TV programmes and films, so his skills had developed, and his dream grew bigger. Turned out that he could do it.

I remember many times, I would watch a TV programme or a series and watch the credits come up at the end and see his name. Things like that bring a smile on your face.

The company was becoming very successful, but then again, change happened. A large company bought them out, and this company did not want this young man's department. There were nine people in the department who were made redundant. What were they to do now that the company did not want their side of the business?

They still had their contacts, and they had a good record. Nature's Power is there for them if they are willing to summon it, just like you. Nature's Power will find a way for you. Belief is the key.

So, a mastermind group of nine decided to start their own company. Is that an easy job? No sir. They needed an office and equipment, and in London, it's all expensive. But they were dreaming big enough and weren't counting facts.

These nine people borrowed money from everywhere to get started. They owned the company. Difficult - yes. Hard times - yes. Struggled - yes. Self-doubt - yes. Hard work and long hours - also yes. They were at it with persistence, will, and belief.

Today, nearly all their loans are paid back, and two years ago, they won their first Oscar. Do you think they are known in the industry now? You bet! How do I know this? That young man is my son-in-law.

Let me tell you another story the great Napoleon Hill once wrote many years ago. He said there was once a father who finally had a baby son. The father was over the moon, ecstatic. The doctor called the father in and told him, "Your son is nice and healthy, but he was born without ears. He will never hear. He does not have the equipment to hear. They did not form in him inside the womb."

The father said he was sorry to hear that his son had no ears, but he did not accept that. He said that his son would hear. The doctor replied it was impossible. The father said was adamant, "My son will hear." The father kept hold of that picture that his son would hear one day, with passion and excitement.

Knock, knock, knock, the Kango hammer of life kept hammering away, blocking out people's opinions. "My son will hear," and the father kept that vision strong, against all opposition. Years later, the son miraculously retrieved 50% hearing.

You see, nature works in powerful ways. The body can change things when there are suggestion and belief repeating into the subconscious mind. The father did not stop believing and kept repeating to his baby son, even when he was asleep, "You are going to hear." If positive pictures are continuously repeated, the subconscious will deliver Nature's Power.

And guess what, that boy was Napoleon Hill's own son. He believed undoubtedly that repeating the picture you want would make it happen.

We have a negative voice and a positive voice within us. We talk to ourselves 90% of the time. Which voice do you think the governor in your head? If you have a small pebble and you drop it in one side of a pond, and someone else drops a bigger pebble on the other side, the ripples will meet in the middle, but the bigger ripples will overcome the smaller ones, gobble them up. The bigger ones will reach the other side, and the smaller ripples will vanish, and neither will reach their destination.

That is what happens in your subconscious mind. The side that wins is the one that gets repeated the loudest and the most often and with total belief. We all use Nature's Power for or against ourselves. To make it work *for* us, keeping the positive thoughts the strongest and keeping hold of that dream is the key. It is much easier to think negatively and let life ride you. It's easy for you to be part of someone else's dream and let life control you. Let someone else steal your dream. They will decide where you live when you can have a holiday, how much money you earn. If you don't follow your dream, you will have to follow someone else's.

Someone else's opinion will determine your future if you don't take the reins to your life. You will be like a ship without a captain to steer it. You will be taken wherever the wind and tide take you. You either pay the price of success, or you will pay for failure and regret for the rest of your life. So I say, shape your own future or someone else will. Be the chess player, not the piece. Be the player on the pitch, not the supporter in the crowd.

We are all participating in the game of life. We only have one crack at this, and there are no replays. No second goes. What do you want out of your life? Do you want to go to your grave with the music still in you? Then follow what I am telling you to do.

***

In September 1941, a young 19-year-old Naval Officer got washed overboard at 4 am. He knew nobody would realise he's in the water until the next watch at 8 am. This Navy vessel was not in the normal shipping lanes. It had left Africa. This young man did not know about Nature's Power. Managing to keep his head above water, he took off his dungarees, tied a knot in the bottom of the legs, let the wind go in and used them as a life jacket.

Now, remember, he did not know the power of nature, but as a young child with a normal upbringing, he had been given hints along the way. This young man believed in God. He said to himself, God will save me, and I will be found. He kept repeating it: knock, knock, knock, like a Kango hammer tapping on. He held on to hope and belief, utmost faith. He kept saying it over and over again. Huge waves were hitting him, he had saltwater in his mouth, but he kept repeating it.

What is remarkable about this true story is that a cruise ship was travelling in the African shipping lane, and for some reason, the captain decided to change its course. Later, the captain said he didn't know why he had changed it to the Spanish lane. Something had told him to, and there they found a young lad in the sea, bobbing about miles from anywhere. He was in the sea for eleven hours but was finally saved. His persistence paid off.

You must believe in something or you will fall for everything.

As I said previously, I wrote down how I wanted my life to be and re-read my story every night for one year. In four years, I had achieved everything I had written down.

Remember I said when I was learning to be a manipulating therapist? I visualised people waiting in my Reception room and lying on my couch? This thing works.

I've read hundreds of self-help and motivational books by different personalities, they all write in their own way, and they all write different stories, but in every single book, there is the same secret, the same power: Nature's Power.

I would suggest my readers to read "How to Become a Millionaire" by Mark L. Alch. It contains stories of very successful people from different countries, different backgrounds, each story is different. Very few of these successful people had an education - but the one thing they all had in common was they *believed*. They pictured success, even when some went bankrupt, they came back even stronger and had the same common trait. They pictured success, living with an "I will" attitude, hard work and belief.

Are you an "I will" or an "I won't" person? You choose.

Can you imagine a four-lane motorway? Two of the lanes are for the "I won't" people, and they have to reverse around the motorway because they like to look backwards and refuse to change or have fears with a follow-the-leader attitude.

Can you imagine their confusion? The head-to-toe traffic jams, the crashes, blockades not moving for hours, running out of petrol. Are they heading towards happiness? Are they feeling well and motivated? Or are they angry, hating and arguing?

This is most people's lives. They have lost the dream and given up on life. They have died on the inside and are waiting for their body to catch up. Waiting, waiting, waiting. Just surviving this life and just keeping their heads above water. Just getting by and worried for the future, worried for their children, worried if the mortgage goes up, dreading the bills coming in and paying off their credit cards. Hoping they don't lose their jobs.

Worry upon worry, is this a good life? Are these people happy inside? Have they given up on their dreams? More importantly... *Is this you?*

On the other side of the motorway are the "I will" people. They are going forward on a clear road. They are on their way to their destination. You know what is amazing about this wonderful life of ours? You can join this lane, and it's free, and you can join at any age.

Look at Ray Kroc in his late fifties. He was not in good health, but that did not stop him from starting McDonald's. He went in with belief and hard work. Colonel Sanders, in his sixties, started Kentucky Chicken, again, with belief and hard work.

If you have a dream and are passionate about it, you must be willing to work hard for that belief. You must keep a strong will to remove the doubters out of your head. The body keeps going forward while you set six-monthly, yearly, two yearly, or five-year goals. The mind does not grow old. The mind controls the body, and the subconscious mind does not know truth or fiction.

While you keep setting the goals and keep thinking ahead with belief, the subconscious mind does not know age. It is only when you keep thinking back that the subconscious mind knows you are getting old and tells you it's time to wind down. Some men do this early when they retire, and most die within five years because they only look back with regret. The mind controls the body, but most allow the body to control the mind.

It's like the tail wagging the dog if you think about it.

Be warned of Nature's Power. It can be used for the wrong reasons: for power and greed, can turn out to be unethical and hurtful.

Hitler knew of Nature's Power too. He used it on TV, radio, posters: knock, knock, knock, repeating the slogans for his own needs. Kings and queens, leaders around the world, Stalin, Mussolini, the Egyptians, they all understood Nature's Power and used it to their advantage. Their decisions sometimes were not in the people's best interest. The great thing about Nature's Power is that if you use it to hurt people or for an unethical purpose, Nature gives you the same back. Hence, it is in everyone's best interest to make sure they use Nature's Power for good.

Advertising companies understand the art of repeating the same slogan every day. Coca Cola is so well-known around the world, but they still advertise. If they were to stop, people would start to drink something else almost overnight.

A company brings out a new product, and that company knows that with continued promotion and marketing of that product, people will start buying. You have seen this happen. This product will be on the TV, every time the adverts are on. Every day you see it. It starts to drop into the subconscious, and you go to the shops, and you see the product on the shelves. You say to yourself *That* product is there. When you go to the shops again, you look for it to see if it's still there. Next week you see it again on the TV. You see it in the papers. You keep seeing it until you buy it; it is because you have seen it so many times that you want it.

So repetition is the key for the things you want in your life. If you want to change things in your life, change your circumstances, go for the good things in life. Eat at the table of abundance. You can, just by keeping the picture in your subconscious like an advertisement and make it happen.

One person can't change the world, but each one of us can change our little world around us, to contain happy, positive people. If we all try to do that, the world will become a better place. Our God-given right is to be happy. Don't let anyone steal your dreams. Let no one's opinion determine your future. Your future is rosy - just believe it.

You might just be working in a factory or an office, or any job where you are employed. Your ambition might be to be the manager one day or be the owner, or even start your own business. You might not even have a job at the moment. Just picture it and act as if you already have that job. Just picture and believe and repeat every day, and it *will* be yours. Be happy at work, smile. If you start at 9 am, then begin at 08:50 am. Don't turn up at 9 am and then go and get a coffee.

Don't be a clock-watcher either. If you finish at 5 pm, leave at 5:15 pm. If the company has a downturn, and the manager has to thin down the staff, the clock-watchers are the first to go. Most employees are just there for the money and believe they are helping the boss become rich. No, the boss provides the building and the tools for you! You work for yourself. You're not sucking up to the boss. You are working on you.

Another key is to compliment people at work. Always smile, be good to the young people, help them to be kind, give your time to the young people who have just started because that young person one day might be a judge at your driving offence hearing. By looking well, happy and healthy, giving your best every day, and keep strengthening the picture of your success, you will be the manager one day or even own the company. You will get that special job you have always wanted. Nature's Power works like a law. It never lets you down. What you expect is what you get. Find out all you can about the company and show interest in who you are working for.

Always be first to do something for someone. You will be surprised by what happens. Believe; the job you have now is only a stepping stone, and enjoy the trip.

Find good out of your work. Anything you want is available and attainable. Everyone has aspirations. It might be taking up a new hobby or sport. Whatever it is, just write it down, be it big or small. Read it every night, and it will be yours - just believe.

I can now go anywhere in my car. In busy car parks or on the streets, ten minutes before I arrive, I picture pulling into that car park, and as I pull in, a car is pulling out of a space just for me. It works every time. Just picture it and believe it. Your life will feel easier.

There will be hard times. They are given to you to make you stronger. Nature's Power can see that sometimes you might be heading the wrong way. Trust in Nature's Power to direct you. The world is your oyster. Make your world and the people in your world happy. Leave a mark when you leave this life. "That the powerful play goes on, and you may contribute a verse," as Whitman said. Have no regrets. When you are happy inside, happy things happen outside. When you are picturing good things, an opportunity will always arrive. Always have your sail up, ready for the wind of opportunity. You only have one life, so make it count.

We all use Nature's Power, so make sure you use it for *you*. Is it hard work being positive? Yes, it takes very hard work to keep the negative out of your head, and it's a life-long job. Is it worth it? You bet it is.

All you have to do is picture your success: repeat, repeat, knock, knock, knock. Like the Kango hammer, hammering a nail into wood, you keep hitting until it's in.

It is that easy.

However, we don't make it easy for ourselves. Let us in the next chapter, cover the four things which will steal your dreams and make you live with the disease called regret.

Joke

I had a leaflet come through the door the other day. It said you can have sex at 80.

I thought that's great, I only live at 79. Not far to walk home.

Your Notes

Chapter 9: The Greatness in Every Child

If you have former failings, they have success written all over them.

As I've kept saying, when we are born, we have two fears: the fear of falling and the fear of loud noises. By the time we are three, we develop many fears. When we are seven, we are hardwired to the way we think and with all the things we fear, which is then compounded by children at school and teachers.

Parents tend to give throw-away comments to their kids; that too, I have mentioned earlier. If you don't remember, go back to Chapter 1. Kids are said 'no' to more than 'yes'. And then my own father called me Knob so, go figure. Children from three years old or even earlier, hear and understand the rows that parents have. At school, we get stuck with nicknames, or we get bullied. You may have had teachers saying to you things such as, "You will never amount to much." Parents say, "You are useless, you're an idiot, just so clumsy".

Most people don't do it right, but bringing up children is probably the most rewarding job in the world, undoubtedly the toughest too. As parents, we need to teach our children right from wrong and incorporate good manners into their personalities. When you need to correct them, use the "custard cream" method. Praise them on the good thing they've done that day before you correct or criticise them for the bad. Then praise them again.

This is a great method that you can apply even with adults. Never tell them they can't do something, but explain why if it is likely to hurt them. Show them that you care for their well-being more and are not infringing upon their 'freedom' to do a thing.

Encourage them if it is to lay a grounding for their future. Always praise and encourage, never put them down. Never correct them in public. Minimise their fears and tell them they can reach the stars. If they don't, they will at least hit the moon, and you will be proud parents. If you want your kids to succeed, you must succeed first. Lead by example. Find out what they are good at. Everyone has been given a gift - find out what theirs is. Take my word for it, the best thing you can give your children is your time, not money nor material goods.

This is an average upbringing that happens with Nature's Power, giving these children hints. But what about the abused children? Their early life experiences create massive fears, their subconscious mind gets filled with the trauma others, and especially adults, have injected in them. These kids start further back than the rest.

Some will grow and become successful in their own right. They learn what the great Tony Robbins says, which hit me right between the eyes the first time I heard him say it, "Things are done *for* us, not *to* us, and when you understand that, you are free."

Some of these kids will grow and help others. Some will be abusers in the future because this gets passed on for generations.

Children who don't have parents, children in orphanages, have more fears than other children. They have no self-esteem and no self-confidence. These children start further back, but they can come through. All have the potential to be stars, though some of them will go ahead to become these stars. Some will be great leaders in their field because they use Nature's Power.

With my son Kane, I left when he was quite young, but thankfully, I was with him every weekend and three nights during the week. I was worried for him, living in a split family. I always told him how good he was, how much I loved him and still tell him that today, even though he is now in his twenties. I constantly fed him positivity.

One day when he was little, we were watching a Cup Final on the TV, and the match went into extra time. Liverpool won 4-3.

Robbie Fowler, a Liverpool forward, made an overhead kick, and it went straight into the roof of the net. My son Kane, who loved football, said, "I want to learn how to do an overhead kick into the back of the net." We went out onto the pitch in the garden, and we started. I showed him how to do it; it all starts with keeping your eyes on the ball. I chipped the ball in, and away he cheered.

He kept trying and missing. He couldn't get the timing right. One time he connected with the ball, and it hit him in the face. Though he had tears in his eyes and his nose was bleeding, he kept on trying. I said, "Kane, it's getting late, boy; you should be in bed now, and it's getting dark." He said, "Dad, I'm not going to bed until I can do this."

He started to get the hang of it with his timing and body shape, but he would not stop until he hit that net and scored. When he did it, he said, "Right, Dad, I will go to bed now." I knew from that point, my boy understood the power of passion and belief. Another thing I understood that day.

Every child has greatness. It's up to us adults to help them find it.

***

I recommend you to read a book called "Afraid" by Sharon McGovern. It's a heart-rending true story of this little girl who was severely abused and raped regularly by her stepfather from the age of 4 to 17. Her childhood was ruined. What chance did this little girl have for a healthy future? But then she began to understand things are done *for* you and not *to* you.

I can hear you say, "What? How can this little girl feel that this was done *for* her?" Because now, this bestseller is going to be a film, but more importantly, she now speaks about her traumatic childhood and helps hundreds of victims get through theirs. We need more people like Sharon McGovern.

You see, our subconscious mind is like a filing cabinet. Everything that has happened to us is stored, good or bad. The off-the-cuff comments, negative or positive, are there, all of them in a file. We constantly pull the filing cabinet drawer open. At the front of the drawer are happy memories. Call them brightly coloured files. We love those memories. However, at the back of the drawer are the black files. We do not open the drawer far enough to let these files out because we bury them.

It is when you are in your deepest sleep that the black files come out. That is when you wake up in the morning depressed, sad or angry, and you don't know why. That is why some adults can't remember their childhood, but decades later, are still haunted by the black files. These files will block your future and your happiness. They will stop you from reaching your potential. But it doesn't matter how old you are, you can remove these files and flush them.

Start repeating, "I will remove those black files." Every day, repeat this with belief.

Write down your fears. What is stopping you from being happy? Take a pen and paper to bed at night and keep repeating every day, I will remove those black files, and one by one, they will come forward. When they do, write them down and, harder still, tell people—writing and telling sets you free.

There are great hypnotherapists out there who do fantastic work.

I highly recommend seeing Tony Robbins speak. He does four-day seminars around the world each year. It costs money, but I promise you, it will be the best investment you will ever make. When you walk out of there, you will have the tools and belief to set you free.

No matter how old you are, what happened to you as a child affects you today, whether you are aware of it or not. Remove those black files, make peace with them, accept yourself, understand that things are done *for* you, and be free.

Joke

Pete the serial flasher was thinking of retiring, but he's gonna stick it out for another year…

Your Notes

Chapter 10: Your Partner

When one member of the couple farts and you both laugh uncontrollably, that's when you have met your soulmate.

Your partner will complete you or compete against you.

Behind every successful man or woman, there is a very successful woman or man. You need a cheerleader. You need to be their hero. And that is your partner.

Laughter, love, happiness in the house, you both need to be singing from the same page. Through my long career so far, I have met hundreds of couples who walk around in quiet desperation. They have changed. There is no love at the table. They have different interests. You must have seen these couples on holiday. They don't speak to each other throughout the trip. Many couples say they only stay together because of the children. They only stay together because of the money. They stay together because of what they might lose. They don't realise they have already lost their future and happiness. They harm the kids further. You are better living in a tent and happy. When they have grown apart but are still living together, that's when people have affairs.

If a shire horse can pull one ton, two shire horses pulling together can pull three tons. It's a fact. That is how a couple works together. Your partner should be your soul mate for life. Some find their soul mate on the first try. Others, like me, take many failed relationships to find my soulmate. I know if I treat her like a queen, she will treat me like a king.

Robin Williams said it right: "I used to think the worst thing in life is to end up all alone. It's not. The worst thing in life is to end up with people who make you feel alone." Since my marital life is all before you, you can tell I have had bad relationships with those who have made me feel alone or have competed with me. This is not to say that I was flawless. Never. It's just our compatibility didn't match. We weren't bad people, just bad together.

That's why we should choose a partner who is good for *us* - not good for your parents, not good for your image, not good for your bank account.

Choose someone who is going to make your life emotionally fulfilling.

There is a difference between someone who wants you and someone who will do anything for you. Be with someone who would drive six hours to spend just an hour with you, and then be that person for your partner too.

Surround yourself with people who don't suck the positive out of you. People with whom talking every day with a positive attitude solves all your problems or at least the more pressing one.

If you and your partner take time every day to set goals together, dream together, there will be happiness and love permeating in the home. You hate being away from each other, you are backing each other, supporting each other, you are happy that the kids are happy. That's how the relationship with your partner needs to be like. You love each other's company. If one of you wants to try a new adventure, you support and back them to the hilt.

If someone keeps making you miserable, let them go. Some people will never change. You have to accept that and move on.

Some will talk to you in their spare time. Others will *make* time to talk. Some will make you dread going home. Others can't wait for you to get home. You choose which one you want.

Do you want to be in a relationship where you both put each other down? Talk badly to your friends about your partner. Where there's no love at the table? Where you can't talk without arguing, and you keep hitting on the bad points? If this is the case, then you're putting your partner down. I can tell that you have probably even stopped complimenting each other.

If reading these lines, you felt a strong sense of relatability, it is time to walk. It's also time to walk if you can't figure out where you stand with your partner.

Don't let the person who does not love you keep you from the one who will. Get out of the bond.

If this is your relationship, it has got to stop for you to be happy in life, to succeed in your dreams and goals. Remember:

A partner must complete you, not compete against you.

If they are not completing you, they are competing against you. Funny as it may be, but in my opinion, when one member of the couple farts and you both laugh uncontrollably, that's when you have met your soul mate. That's the standard you should aim for with your partner.

Joke

The postman had the shock of his life the other day. I don't know whether it was seeing my naked body, or that I knew where he lived.

Your Notes

Chapter 11: The Crab Basket

Misery loves company

Entertain a scenario for me.

A big round basket with a hole in the top gets lowered down by a rope to the sea bottom. A crab will come along, climb up the basket and drop in. He is on the sea bed in the basket. He is secure in there. He can see all around him.

This is wonderful. Another crab comes along, drops in the basket. He settles down, and he is secure. Then another crab drops in, then another. The first crab thinks, "Fuck this!" It is getting overcrowded, so he tries to get out. Why not, there's a big hole at the top.

He starts to climb up and out, only to be pulled back by the other crabs. He tries again and gets pulled back. Every time he tries, he gets pulled back. If he continues, the other crabs will tear his legs off.

Does this remind you of a situation yourself? What moral do you get out of this? That misery loves company. Do you give thought to what is it that stops you from getting happy and successful in the life that you are destined for?

The point I am trying to make you think about is that when you decide to follow your dreams for a happy, healthy life, and you start using Nature's Power for *you*, you may find that your friends, siblings, parents, cousins, neighbours, even your partner, may end up dragging you back down into the basket.

The contrary may happen too, though. When you decide to follow your dreams for a happy, successful life, some will encourage you, and that is great. It is these people that you should make your tribe with. The others, those who pull you away from success, will drag you down to the bottom of the crab basket with them. When you put your head up above the crowd, you cop the rotten tomatoes.

These are deflated individuals who have stopped using Nature's Power and cannot let you use it either now. You will have to pull away from them. They want you to stay at their level. They like pity parties. They are continually negative. They do not want you to succeed, but I know you want to.

Every time they speak, a negative morsel falls out of their mouth. They tell you that it won't work. They say things like:

"You can't do that."

"I know someone who did that, and it didn't work."

I had a former wife who said to me, "Why don't you just be normal?" I said, "I am being normal."

I had a friend we called Sunshine because every time he went out the door, the room brightened up. Surround yourself with positive people like Sunshine, who help and encourage you. If you are with negative people, the Doom and Gloom Brigade, they will drag you down into the Crab Basket. They think the world owes them. They are in this negative state because of someone else: their boss, the government, their parents. They say things such as, "I'm always unlucky, and nothing ever goes right for me."

Cause and effect. They are where they are today because of decisions they made earlier. They use Nature's Power against themselves because of their beliefs. They have the biggest disease of mankind: Regret.

Joke

I gave the mother-in-law something shiny for Christmas. It goes 0 to 150 in two seconds. Scales.

Your Notes

Chapter 12: Leave a Legacy for Yourself

Live for the nights you'll never remember with the friends you'll never forget.

What power there is in chasing the opposite sex! A dog does not know he has got a flea when he is on the hunt.

Young men are controlled by the small head. It is only when they are mature that they put that incredible power into their success in life. Just like with a dog, when they are in the hunt, there is no stopping them.

History has shown us that very successful men have been destroyed because of their small head. They use Nature's Power for the hunt. They become "I will" people, but for everything else, they become "I won't" people and use Nature's Power against them.

These four things are tied together. Can you see why most people fail to be happy, healthy and successful and are not at the table of abundance? They drift through life, playing out the string. They are dead on the inside and just waiting for the body to catch up. Here we are, all using Nature's Power *for* us or *against* us; it's your choice. We can change at any time at any age. We can see the things which hold us back now. The four things, locked together, stop us from eating at the table of happiness and abundance.

None of us is getting out alive. We have one life, get one crack at it. Can you imagine lying on your death bed with regret? "I wish I had done this and done that."

Embrace change. It's exciting! When you ride life, life is not riding you. Instead of putting it off, let's start today with small goals. Write down exactly what you want from this life.

Start to remove the negative people from your life. You still love them, but they don't align with your life goals. Start spending time with positive, like-minded people. Read every day, choose a self-help book. Start to take charge of those negative thoughts as they come into your mind; remove them and say out loud, "I'm now in control." *Knock, knock, knock,* persistent, positive pictures.

As you start to spend time with positive people, you will begin to understand that they uplift you. They give you energy. Negative people, on the other hand, are like human ticks; they suck the energy out of you and give nothing back. You spend half an hour with a human tick, and you feel drained. The human tick only takes and never gives.

You spend time with a positive person, you feel energised and happy.

You must have noticed at a gathering or party, the positive people have got loads of people around them. The negative people are on their own.

You don't want to be among those people. Start picturing instead how and who you want to be. It doesn't matter where you are, maybe today you have no job and you're broke. Start reading, picturing who you want to be all the time with belief, and Nature's power will do the rest.

You don't need any qualifications or experience. Read the book '*How to Think Like a Millionaire*' by Mark Fisher, and you will realise that most of the people mentioned in the book had no great education or qualifications. They just thought about success and followed a dream with belief. Some have even gone bankrupt and became millionaires again. You must have wondered why some people succeed in life while others who put more efforts don't. Some people think they are lucky. But what they are doing is using Nature's Power for *them*. Luck just means labouring under the correct knowledge.

What have you got to lose? What you have been doing doesn't work.

Follow what successful people do. The great Jim Rohn said, "Success leaves clues."

If you are nervous or shy, this is what you need to write down:

"I'm going to be more outgoing, smile at everyone, and I'm going to be positive."

Write down how you want your life to be. Read it out loud every day with belief, passion and will, all on your own and do not tell anyone. This WILL happen. It cannot fail. You are working with nature.

People will start to come your way. People you have never met before will come into your life. That is when opportunities will arrive. Do not dither but jump straight in, even if you don't know anything about it. Jump in and learn along the way. Nature's Power will direct you. Have faith, belief and willpower.

You can't get to second base with one foot still on first base. Have the attitude of "I would rather die trying than lose."

Many years ago, a king and his army sailed to a country to conquer it. They anchored the ships, and the army went ashore. When they were all on land, the king told his general to burn all the ships. When the general asked why, the king told him, "Because there is no way back when the going gets tough. They can't run, they have to win, they have to face the odds."

Generally, when life is threatened, people will always succeed.

The great Tony Robbins said, "If you want to succeed in this great life, you must burn your fucking boats."

It doesn't matter what comes your way, be resourceful and be determined.

Nature will lead and help you. You will come up against things you have never done before, but jump in and get on with it. Ninety per cent of what you worry about never happens. Five per cent you can solve, and the other five per cent you can do nothing about, so don't worry and move on. Nothing can stop passion, belief and a strong will.

I remember a few years ago it happened to me - I came up against something that I had never seen before and never dealt with previously.

I had just finished with a client and was going to have something to eat when I heard my name being called. It was my dad calling from the bathroom.

I opened the door, and there he was, standing up, hands on the wall, with shit all over his hands, arms, and all over the toilet seat. He was in his pants, trousers and socks. It was all over the floor, and the smell was horrendous. I wanted to run, but I closed the door. I faced up, put on rubber gloves and with a big black plastic bag, I went in.

I started to take his shoes, socks, trousers and pants off. I was heaving. The smell! There was a pile of shit on the mat, and I can only describe that his arse was like a cement mixer. Just churning out pile after pile. As I led him into the shower, it was still coming out like a cement mixer. It was the worst half-hour of my life, but I had to do it. I had shit all over me.

I cleaned Dad up, put him in his bedroom, cleaned the bathroom, and everything went into a black bin bag. Then Julie came home from work. She had her own private care company. I told her what had happened, and she laughed, saying she dealt with that every day.

I was going to throw the black bag away, but she promptly started to wash the shitty clothes and mats. To Julie, it was nothing but an everyday thing. You see, when you make doing the difficult things everyday work, you make it easy for yourself through repetition. I now know that carers are not paid enough.

***

On your new journey, you will meet rejection, roadblocks, failure, but you are now using Nature's Power for yourself. Nature always finds a way. Enjoy every challenge with passion, belief and will. You're learning with every failure. You're getting stronger. Your life is getting better every day, and you're feeling happier. You're on your journey of fulfilment.

Life is for giving. Give more, and you will find deeper fulfilment. When you give, it comes back to you. Not necessarily money as there is a greater payment than that.

When I was a young man, I went out for some shopping. Near a DIY shop, I saw an old lady struggling with a large can of paint. She struggled onto her mobility scooter and put her tin of paint into her basket, but the paint fell out and onto the path. It burst open, and paint went everywhere. I took the paint tin from her and went into the DIY shop. They came out with some paper and cleaned her scooter and the pavement.

I asked the man if he could give her another tin of paint. He said she would have to pay for another one as the paint is expensive. The poor old lady was so upset. She had been saving for months. Her nephew was coming to paint her lounge. I went back into the DIY shop and asked, "How much is that paint?" He told me, and I took my money out. There was enough in my wallet, in fact, I had a pound left after the expenditure. I ran out to the lady and gave her the bucket of paint.

She looked at me with tears in her eyes and said she couldn't afford another tin of paint. I said, "No, it's a gift from me."

She said I didn't know her, and I said, "I know, but you are a person in need, and we should all help other people." She drove away smiling and happy. I felt ten feet tall. I only had a pound left for my shopping, but that didn't matter. What I felt was the biggest payment ever.

It made me feel great about myself and my life. For me, this feeling is the greatest payment - even the Inland Revenue can't take that - it's priceless. These gave me two lessons:

Give when you can't afford it.

Give your time to others in need.

When you are enjoying your life with happiness, all I ask is that you teach others as many as you can. Leave a mark for others to follow. Leave a legacy in your world.

In these pages is the key to your happiness and success in your life. You pay now for your happiness, or you pay for failure and live with regret.

Go on, change your life and that of others.

Use Nature's Power for *you* and discover a new world of happiness.

Joke

And the Lord said unto John, "Come forth and you will receive eternal life."

But John came fifth and won a toaster.

Your Notes

Chapter 13: Let's Wrap It Up

The power within you is greater than the power within this world.

So here it is, nice and simple. In Part 1, I've told you how I came to realise, through personal experience, that life doesn't just happen to you; you can make it happen. I made some mistakes and some decisions, and I saw the consequences of those and realised there is no one else to blame for the bad or the good that comes out of it.

Now I will tell you how this works.

What you think about or focus on all day long will happen. What the mind of man can conceive and believe will happen. It is your choice. You are in control of your thoughts, whether *for* you or *against* you. Start today and start eating at the table of abundance. It is yours - claim it.

If it is a car that you want, go and test-drive your car. Have a picture of it which you look at every day. Imagine it is already yours. Every day, imagine you are sitting in your car: smell the new leather, feel the steering wheel. It is yours. Act as if you already have the car. You are just waiting for it to be delivered. You imagine this every morning and before you go to bed. You imagine with excitement and passion, and this makes you happy. Sit with your eyes closed. Feel the excitement and passion for your new car. When you are happy and excited, passion is flowing through your body - when that is happening, negative thoughts can't get in.

Be the doorman of your mind. You do not let negatives in. Do not worry about how you are going to pay for it. Your job is to visualise with passion and belief. Nature's power will send you the money.

If your dream is to just pay your bills, you must get rid of that thought. Bills hold a negative connotation and bring stressful energy when you think like that. If you are thinking of bills, Nature's Power will give you bills. Nature's Power gives you what you ask for.

Think wealth, think money, and you will have loads of it. You can pay any bill. Your thoughts will attract or repel money. Act as if you have loads. Even write out a cheque for any amount that makes you happy in your name. Big or small, the money is already there, just waiting for you to ask. Put the cheque with the picture of the car. Act as if you have both. The car is on your drive, and the money you have asked for is in your account.

Rather than thinking bills, imagine cheques coming through the letterbox.

It may be a new kitchen that you need. Go and get it planned. Put the plan and a picture of it up with the car and cheque. Imagine you're in your kitchen, cooking. It may be a new bathroom. Anything you want is yours, and you have to vividly imagine to have it. Otherwise, Nature would not put that into your mind. Nature's power gives you your dreams because they are yours. Just claim them.

Look around at the people who already have all the things that you want, the things that will make you happy. Why have they got those things? Because they believed and understood Nature's Power. What you ask for with belief, excitement and passion is yours.

Be thankful for what you already have. Be happy with what you have. Say thank you every day for your life, and Nature's Power will give you more. If you are resentful and jealous, Nature's Power will give you more of that because what you think about, nature will give you.

Have you ever thought when you turn on the radio, music just comes on? How does that get there? Where does it come from? There's a radio studio somewhere with a DJ playing the music. How does it get to your radio in your home? How do you speak to someone on your mobile phone who lives miles away and with no wires attached? Your TV has pictures and music, laughter and talking. How does that get onto your screen, into your home, from another country?

Radio waves, sound waves and video signals are sent from big transmitter towers and bounced off satellites that reach your TV or radio. You cannot see these waves, but obviously, they are there. Turn on your radio, and music is there. You know this. Your phone rings, and you talk. You believe though you can't see the waves, you know that they are there. What about electricity? You can't see it, but you believe. You flick a switch, and the light comes on. You cannot see electricity, but you know it is there and it's powerful.

Our mind is the most powerful transmitter. It sends out powerful vibrating waves and attracts anything you ask for.

You don't question it when you turn on a light or your TV. When you get on a plane, you turn right and find your seat. You don't turn left to check the pilot out. You have faith and belief. He knows what he is doing and will get you there safely and into the right airport. When you sit down, do you check out the seat first, or do you sit straight down? You have the belief that it is safe.

We take many things for granted because we believe. Turn on the radio - music. Turn on the TV - pictures. You believe. You can't see the waves, but they are there.

Success and happiness are there waiting for you. You have the most powerful transmitter in the world, sending out vibrating waves and giving you what you ask for in abundance.

You can't see Nature's Power, but it is there.

Like the radio and TV, you have buttons for changing the channels. Nature's Power is the same. Just tune in to the right channel: positive thoughts, with happiness, passion and belief, and you will have everything and more. You get exactly what you ask for.

If you say, "I can't, or I don't think that would work for me," you are right, and it won't work for you. Change your language. You are hung by your tongue. When you start believing in Nature's Power, you will be on a different plane of thinking. You can then tap into the infinite intelligence of wisdom that is out there from people who are long gone but have made their spirit and wisdom available for everyone.

If you have a challenge that you need to solve, go to bed and close your eyes. In the morning, with 100% belief, Nature's Power will give you the answer. Hand it over to nature.

Over the centuries, men and women have used this power to receive success and happiness. If you are not happy, you are unhappy with your job, your home, your spouse or partner, or you haven't got a job, and you are always ill. Whatever you are doing will not be working. The first sign of madness is always doing the same things and expecting a different result. If things are not to your liking or you are unhappy, you can change your thoughts. What have you got to lose? Nothing. You have everything to gain.

Believe in Nature's Power 100% for two years, starting now, and it will surprise you like how it surprised me.

***

This is how most people live their lives:

We have a very large fish tank, and in there, we put in a pike fish which loves eating other fish. It has big teeth, and it's strong. We placed a strong glass partition in the middle of the tank from top to bottom. On the other side of the partition, we put in small goldfish, which are quite happy swimming around their half of the tank. The pike sees them, and he is hungry. He chases them, but he keeps smashing his head on the glass partition. Bang, bang. He is hungry and frustrated, but he keeps trying and keeps banging his head.

Some pike will do this for days or weeks as they are hungry, but then they get despondent, and they are hurting. They can't reach their dream - a simple little goldfish. They lay down and sulk and then give up.

You can then take out the partition and let the goldfish swim around the pike freely. The pike has given up, and he would rather die than try again.

How many people do you know like that? They give up on their dreams and will die with the music still in them.

***

In an old-fashioned pub deep in the country, a big old dog lay in front of the log fire, and every ten to twelve minutes, he would cry out and then go back to sleep. A man asked the pub landlord why that dog cried out every now and then and went back to sleep? The landlord said, "He loves that fire, warm and cosy, but where he lays, there is a nail that sticks out of the flooring and sticks into him." The man asked why did the dog not move then? The landlord said, "Perhaps it doesn't hurt him that much."

Do you know people like that? They give up on the dream, their happiness. They moan about everything but can't be bothered any more to move.

If you get a frog and put him in a saucepan, he will sit there very comfortably. He can jump out at any time, but he is happy. Put the saucepan on the stove and fill it with water, and the frog is in heaven as the water gets warm; he is loving his life. He is not going to jump out. The water gets hotter, it starts boiling, and the frog says, "Fuck this, I'm out."

But he gets cooked in the squat, as he took too long to move because he was comfortable.

How many people do you know who get cooked in the squat? They are always saying they are going to change their lives, but they never do. You should not be one of them.

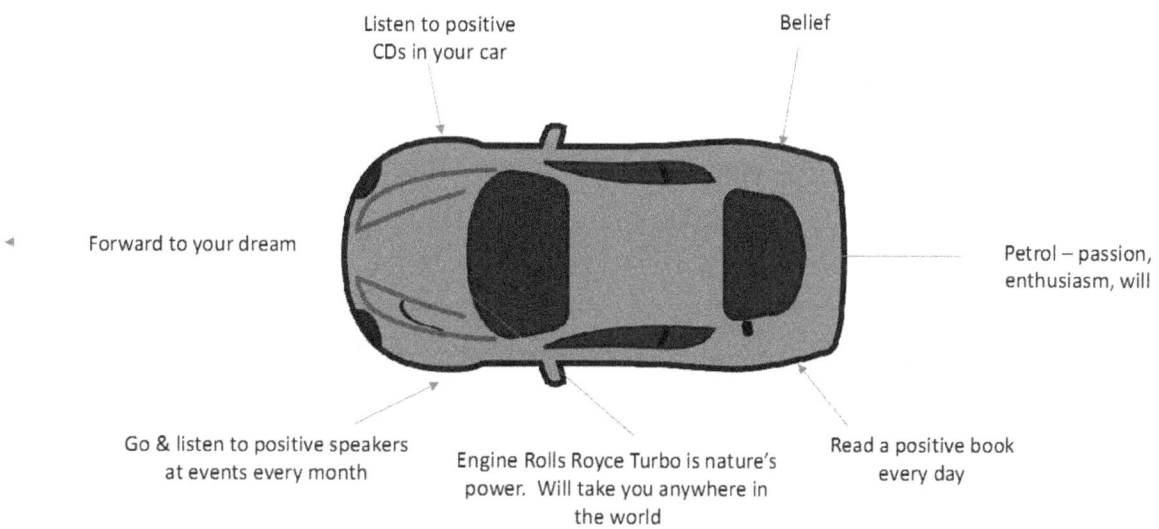

***

Think of a car as your life.

As you can see, I'm no artist, but this is a fair illustration of a sports car with the labels:

Go forward to your dreams. All parts of the car make the whole. Miss one off, and you stop.

Let's look at another example.

If I put down on the floor a scaffold board twelve inches wide and fourteen feet long, nearly everyone could walk along that. If we put it up three feet high, most people could walk along the plank. Now, what if I put another plank on top of the first plank and nailed them together, so now they are twice as thick. We put the boards on top of a 500 ft. tower, across to another 500 ft. tower, and they are ten feet apart. Towers this tall sway with the wind. They are designed to do that. It is windy up there, and the boards are getting icy. Who would walk across the plank to the other side? Remember, one of our first fears as a baby is of falling. I would imagine not many, if any, would cross.

Now, if the dream is big enough, important enough, the facts do not count.

Imagine I'm on the other side, holding your two-year-old daughter by the foot over the edge. I say to you, "If you don't come over the plank to me, I will drop your daughter to her death." How many would come across that plank, save your daughter and rip my head off? How many would say, "I can't! Drop her." Nobody. When the dream is big enough, your fears go, and you use Nature's Power.

***

How many times have you left your house via the front door, and you walk up the road and can't remember shutting the front door? You go back and find it shut. You've done that subconsciously. If you do the same with Nature's power and believe, your dreams will arrive.

Find yourself a mentor or coach. If there is a person you know and would love to be in his position, duplicate 100% what he or she does. For example, if you jumped into a river 50 feet wide and swam across to the other side, you must duplicate this 100% to get to the other side. If you don't, you die.

Nature teaches us change: summer, winter, spring and autumn; night and day, up and down, hot and cold, happy and sad, laughter and crying. We prune shrubs and trees after the frosty season for new growth. We plant seeds in the spring and bulbs. Nothing ever remains the same. The Earth is in constant flux. We must adapt to change. Happy people don't just accept change, they embrace it with excitement and passion. It's a new adventure.

As you go up the ladder of success and happiness, you will have challenges and disasters, but that is nature, to make you stronger to keep getting up that ladder. The higher you climb, the bigger the challenge. You come to a place where you say, "Throw me the challenge!" because you know you can deal with it, and it becomes second nature.

You are now bigger than any challenge. By now, you are halfway up the ladder. Any challenge you get, you can beat it to death with a bag of money. You are halfway there to the table of abundance.

Most people say, "I have tried this power thing, and it doesn't work." They are on the wrong frequency. "I have cast my bread across the waters, and someone nicked it."

No good having a wishbone if it is not backed up by a backbone.

The way we think and the decisions we make determine our future.

Are you going to stand up for your happiness? Spartacus did. The Romans wanted Spartacus, and they chased him down a hillside, and there were many men on the hillside. The Romans approached the men saying they wanted Spartacus. "Tell us who he is and where he is!" The men kept quiet, and the Romans said they would kill everyone unless they told them where he was. Spartacus stood and, with a loud and proud voice, said, "I'm Spartacus!" The Romans moved in, and then there was another shout, and a man stood up, saying, "I'm Spartacus!" The Romans looked, and then another shouted, "I'm Spartacus!" and then another and another.

Are you going to stand up for your family and their future?

***

Revisiting Nature's Law.
It's an old adage, whatever you don't use, you lose. Examples are:

- Ambition - unused, it will disappear
- Faith - unused, it's gone
- Energy - unused, it diminishes
- Vitality - unused, it vanishes
- Feelings - unused, they die

This shouldn't be something you don't already know. For instance, you know well that if you stop using your legs, you lose the power to walk.

Some people think they are worthless. But they already won the race to the egg out of 100,000,000 sperm, so they are special.

Would you sell both your eyes for a million? Would you sell your heart for a million? Would you sell your legs for a million?

Can you see where I am going with this? So far, you are worth more than three million pounds, and I haven't even gotten started.

You were put on this Earth for a reason. As a motivational speaker, Les Brown always said, "There is greatness in you."

Stand up for your right to live in abundance. It is your gift from Nature. Go and claim it.

There are three kinds of people in this world:

> People who make things happen
>
> People who watch things happen
>
> People who say, "What the fuck happened?"

Which one of these are you going to be?

Think about the eagle. What about the eagle, you say? It lives for seventy years, but to reach that age, he has challenges to meet. At forty, his long, strong, flexible talons can no longer grab his prey, which starts to make the eagle hungry. His long, sharp beak has become soft and bendy. The forty-year-old wings become heavy and stick to his chest, which makes it very difficult to fly. He has a decision to make. Live or die.

How many forty-year-old people do you know who refuse to make a change, keep doing the same things and expect a different result? They are in a rut. The only difference between a rut and a grave is timing. They say they are too old and can't change. They are dead inside and waiting for the body to catch up.

The eagle has a decision to make: go through pain or slowly starve to death. If he goes through the pain, he lives for another thirty years. People in their forties only have to think differently and use Nature's Power for the next thirty years to eat at the table of abundance. So it comes down to this piece of wisdom:

Change your thoughts. Change your life.

Eagles are incredible birds. They live at the highest points. If they want to live, they will go through pain, knocking out their beak first, which is so painful. It's like having teeth pulled out with no anaesthetic. Once the beak is out, they wait for it to grow back, so they can start to pull their talons out with their new strong beak. Then they start on the wings, plucking out all the feathers. Can you imagine the pain? They have a dream to live another thirty years, with a renewed body and young again. This process lasts 150 days.

As humans, all we have to do is change our thinking and use Nature's Power. I know which I would prefer to be. Do you?

***

Twenty or so years ago, I met a man they call "The Miracle Man". There were 16,000 people in the Birmingham NIA, or the National Indoor Arena, as it was called then. This made the biggest impression on me ever. What a sensation! I was running the ground floor security, and I was at the edge of the stage. They showed a film about what had happened to this man.

The Miracle Man crashed in his plane, hitting power lines and smashing to the ground. The plane was completely smashed to bits. They got the man out and took him to the hospital, believing he would be dead on arrival. On examination, he had broken his neck, C1 and C2 (which are the top vertebrae next to the skull). His muscles were destroyed, and his diaphragm completely shattered. His spinal cord was damaged severely, paralysing him from the neck down. They put him on a respirator as, without a diaphragm, you cannot breathe. The hospital contacted his family and said they must come because he would not make it through the night… but he did.

They carried out an operation to make him more comfortable, but they expected him to pass away at any time. All this man could do was blink his eyes.

This very emotional film lasted about thirty minutes, and all the audience cried, knowing that the man had unbelievable injuries. It seemed impossible that he would survive, and if he did, he would be a vegetable, and he was only able to blink his eyes.

The film stopped, and everyone was quiet for several minutes. The stage was dark. Then the lights came on, and an announcement was made: "Please welcome Morris Goodman."

This man walked onto the stage with a walking stick. I nearly fell off the stage. The audience screamed, and the noise was incredible. It was theatre at its best. The applause went on forever. People were passing out. We were carrying people out and out there; people were getting sick. I have never seen anything like it. The cheering and clapping seemed to go on and on. With all those injuries, it had seemed impossible, but with will, determination, belief, passion and Nature's Power, all things are possible.

Morris Goodman had the belief that he would walk out of that hospital in eight months, and he did. He still had a dauntingly hard struggle for many years to get his body functioning well, but with belief and Nature's Power, today he is alive and happy and speaks all over the world.

The mind is the most powerful thing in the world, and when it's in tune with Nature's Power, the mind can create and cure anything. You just need belief.

***

We have talked about vital things, but let's go deeper.

The body's cells are formed by the mind. Cells cluster together and form living matter. Every part of our body is formed by cells. Our cells are replaced with new ones every three months. In one year, we have a complete set of young, renewed cells. The mind controls the cells, and the mind is in contact with infinite intelligence: Nature's Power.

So, the mind creates cells.

People have illness and disease, and tumours. The cells of these diseases and tumours are renewed with brand new cells every year, so why are the diseases and tumours still there? Because of our mindset. Negative thoughts towards the disease are keeping it there. Nature's power is doing what you ask of it.

Let's look at this from a different angle.

Say you completely knock down your house to the ground, and nothing is left. You now have the chance to build a new house from scratch, but because you could not be bothered to get new plans. You used the old plans that the house you knocked down was built from. What happens is you end up with the same house. That is what you do when the picture is held in your mind. Nature's Power will give you what you picture.

In my clinic, I need my patients to believe that I am going to remove their pain, and I do as well. With both of us believing, we get the job done. On a few occasions, I have had clients who have been forced to come to the clinic against their partners' will. They tell me I cannot help them. I tell them, "You are completely right. I cannot help you today. There is no charge. Go back to the doctor."

Many years ago, I met a couple called Allan and Barbara Pease. They wrote a best seller called *Body Language.* What a marvellous couple they are. They explain just how important body language is: the way you dress, carry yourself, stand, walk with confidence, all of these things speak volumes about you. If you configure yourself to act as if you are already a millionaire through your body language, you will get there.

All this has to be done before acquiring success. If you are going for an office job, ensure you have a nice pressed suit, a tie (which ends at your belt, not too long and not too short). If you can't get that right, wear a waistcoat. A clean, crisp shirt, polished shoes, black socks - not white as it makes you look like a prat. Smile and always look the interviewer in the eyes. Let them know this is your job.

It's the same with any job interview. Wear what is appropriate for the job. Look crisp, clean and upright, smile, smell good, have your hair in shape. Or you might be going to make a sale, and the same things apply.

What you look like and how you hold yourself speaks so loudly. You may not have said a word yet. What that means is, if you are not looking crisp, clean and sharp, you have lost the job or sale before you open your mouth.

A boy called Thomas Edison brought home a letter from the school, which he was told not to open but to give to his mum. She opened the letter. It said: "I'm afraid that Thomas is not teachable, he is disruptive and mentally short. We have had to expel him from this school." After his mum read the letter, she folded it and put it in her pocket. Thomas asked what the letter said, and his mum replied, "Thomas, you are so above the other children. You are far ahead mentally, and they suggested that you stayed at home with me, and I will teach you." What a mum she was! She was using Nature's Power.

Thomas Edison went on to become the greatest inventor.

When his mum died, he found the letter. He hadn't known he was using Nature's Power. When he read the letter, he used Nature's Power to the full.

Laugh every day and have joy in your heart. Every day, even when disaster strikes.

Seven years ago, I had a wonderful Boxer dog. Flo was her name, and I had her from a pup. I was in the Clinic, and Julie called me into the conservatory. She said, "I think Flo has died." There she was, dead on the floor, and my heart sank. She'd lived a great long life, but it still hurt. My good friend had gone. I picked her up, wrapped her in her blanket and put her in the garage because it was February, late and dark. I said I would bury her in the morning.

I had a troublesome night but woke up early. It was pissing down. Never mind, it had to be done. I first made a box to put Flo in as I didn't want any animal digging her up. Dad and I put Flo into the box, and I screwed the lid on. We carried her down to the shed. She was a big dog, and what with her and the box, this was heavy. Dad said, "When you've dug the grave, let me know, and I will help you lower her into it."

I started to dig, and it was fucking pissing down. In our area, the ground is full of clay, and I wanted to dig very deep so she couldn't be dug up. After two hours, I was down with my head level with the top. It was still pissing down, and the hole was getting full of water, and I couldn't get out of the grave. I then had to dig the steps so I could climb out. I was soaked, and the clay was all over me.

Dad turned up to see how I was getting on, and he got sad, but when he saw me, a smile appeared. He said, "Did you get stuck in that hole?" I said, "Come on, let's get this done," as it was still pissing down. We picked up the box with me walking backwards. Remember, by this point, Dad had had two strokes, so he was tottery. I had left a walkway between the clay I had dug out and the grave so we could lower the box down. I was walking backwards; I went between the clay, and the grave, and Dad was walking forward. As he approached the grave, he tripped on a rhododendron root and, in slow motion, was heading down the grave, head first. The box with Flo in it was on top of my dad, and they were going down the grave.

I don't know how to this day, but I held the box with one hand, grabbed my dad by his shirt collar and dragged him out with the other. He was kneeling on the ground, and I had lowered the box down into the hole by myself. I said, "What the fuck are you doing? Why did you want to get in that fucking hole before Flo?" He was covered head-to-toe in clay, and he was crying. He said, "That made a very sad day into a funny one."

On another occasion - it is quite funny, really - Dad was involved again. My Auntie Olive, Dad's younger sister, had died. This made my dad, one of eleven children, the only one remaining. On the day of the funeral, I had to get Dad's clothes out for him, and he got dressed with my help. I asked him if he needed a belt with those trousers, but he said no, they were fine.

We went to the funeral. He didn't have a lot of use in his hands, and he kept skurfing up his trousers with his wrists, which eventually pulled his shirt out and his boxer pants up. The funeral finished, and we went to my cousin's house for the wake.

Olive had two sons, Michael and Tony. There must have been fifty people in the wake. I sat Dad down in the lounge opposite the food table. He was chatting for hours. He called me over and said, "I want to go now." I found Tracy, Michael's wife, and told her Dad wanted to go now. She said to my dad, "Please take some food with you, John." He picked out some lovely cakes, which she wrapped up.

The two sons, Michael and Tony, were in the lounge saying goodbye, as well as thirty old dears who were sitting down. Dad stood up, holding onto his cakes, and his trousers fell down to his ankles. Tracy and her sister bent down to pull his trousers up. Tracy was in front of Dad, and when she knelt down, she was looking straight at his knob, which was an inch away. His knob was hanging out of his pee hole, and his balls were hanging out of one leg of his pants. Tracey asked me, "Did you not dress him properly today?" By then, I was on the floor, and I couldn't move for the biggest belly laugh, having seen Tracy eyeball to eyeball with my dad's knob. Everyone was laughing, and Michael and Tony thanked my dad for making a very sad day for them, a funny one.

My dad held onto those cakes and did not bother with what was happening. Cakes come first, not the trousers.

***

A young fourteen-year-old wanted to know the secret of success. His dad told him, "Go see your uncle. He is a very successful man." The young lad went to see his uncle, who was sitting on his front porch. He asked his uncle, "How are you doing?"

His uncle replied, "Great, life is fantastic."

"I know," said the boy. "My dad said you are very successful in life, Uncle. He told me you would give me the secret of success."

The uncle said, "You are too young at the moment. Have a glass of pop and some cake."

The boy, now fifteen, went back to his uncle and asked the same things. The uncle gave the same replies, "You're too young, come back when you are sixteen."

When the boy was sixteen, he went back and said, "Uncle, I am sixteen and ready." The uncle said, "OK, follow me." It was a hot summer's day, and both were in shorts. They walked across the uncle's land and came to a lake where they had fished together before. The young lad loved his uncle, and he trusted him to the hilt.

The uncle said, "Right, let's take our shoes off, and we are going to walk into the lake."

The boy said, "Uncle, I thought you were going to teach me the secret of success."

"Be patient, boy," the uncle said. They walked in together.

"Hold my hand," said the uncle, and the boy did. As they got deeper in, up to the boy's shoulders, the uncle, who was 6 ft 6 inches and a big man, pulled the boy close to him, placed a hand on each shoulder and held him under the water.

The boy did not worry at first as it was his uncle. He would not hurt him. He was playing. The uncle kept the boy under the water, and he started to wriggle but could not surface. He was holding his breath and started to struggle, thinking his uncle would let him up in a minute as he must see him struggling. The uncle did not. The boy started to struggle more strongly. He started kicking his uncle and biting his arm. He was getting frantic, going berserk and thrashing everywhere. With one last effort, he pushed his uncle over and got his head above water.

His uncle jumped up, laughing. The boy was crying and coughing. He was scared. How come his uncle was trying to kill him?

The uncle said, "Right, let's get you back and dry you out with a hot cup of tea." They sat on the porch, the boy sipping his tea, still shaking and confused.

The boy said, "Uncle, why did you try to drown me?"

The uncle replied, "You wanted to know the secret of success."

"Yes, Uncle, but what was all that about?" asked the boy.

"The secret of success? You must have a dream," said the uncle, "and a burning desire and belief. In the lake, when I held you down, and you realised I was not going to let you up, that was your dream and burning desire to get a breath. You thought hard and came to a point where you will live or die. You gave everything you had, plus more and you got your dream; you lived. That, my boy, is the secret: you have a dream, a major purpose, and you go for it with everything you have. Rather die than lose. You keep going for the dream until you have it with belief. That my boy is the secret of success in a nutshell."

You see, it's when you want to succeed as badly as you want to breathe that you go the extra mile. That is what gets you success.

Nature's Power dismisses people who want something for nothing. People who won't work but want the goodies. People who would rather rob than work.

We are dealing with Nature here. What you plant, you get. People who want something for nothing get nothing. This is nature's law. If you don't plant in your garden, you get weeds and nettles.

Going the extra mile ensures Nature's Power is working for you. It is mental growth.

Not being a clock-watcher gets you up the ladder of success. Doing more than you are paid for; getting in early, and leaving late makes you indispensable to your employer. You will always have work. You will get to the top of everything you do. This also removes procrastination.

Doing more than you are paid for will always come back to you two-fold, like compounding interest. You will have leverage with your boss because he or she won't want to lose you. Then you will get a pay-raise or get head-hunted by another company. Companies want these people and will pay a premium.

So, when you go that extra mile with a smile, you will never be out of a job. In fact, if you go the extra mile, you will be the boss or own the company in the end.

When you go the extra mile with Nature's power, jobs will come to you.

***

A good friend of mine built a very successful business, working seven days a week until 12 o'clock at night. He started out with no money in his pocket and with nowhere to live. He started handing out leaflets in the High Street all day, every day until his hands were bleeding. He was on a mission, going the extra mile, out every day until his business started working, money started to come in, and he could rent a small cottage. He knew the power of the dream, so he went to a top-class car showroom. His dream was to own a Ferrari, a red one. There in the showroom was his dream. He looked at it, opened the door and sat in the driver's seat. He had old trainers on, ripped jeans and an old jacket. He looked as if he didn't have a tin to piss in.

The well-dressed salesman came up to him and said, "Please, sir, would you get out of the car with those dirty clothes. These cars are for people with money, not for people like you." The young man asked, "How much is this?" The abrupt salesman said, "You will never be able to afford one of these. Stop wasting my time and leave or I will get security to chuck you out." But the young man sat in his dream, and now he had another one to prove that salesperson wrong.

Two years later, my friend went in there again and purposely put old clothes on, so he looked like a down-and-out. There was no red Ferrari in the showroom, so a young man came up to him and said politely, "Can I help you?" My friend said, "Have you any red Ferraris?" The young man said, "Yes, we have one out the back." They went around the back, and there was a nice red Ferrari. The young man said, "Would you like a test drive?" "Yes, please," said my friend.

My friend asked the young salesman how long he had been working there. He said: "Three weeks. The money is poor, but I get a commission. A lot of commission on a car like this." My friend asked the price and said he would be back.

The next day my friend returned and when he entered the car showroom, the older salesman who had asked him to leave two years before because he thought my friend was a chancer was there. My friend asked for the young salesman he was speaking to yesterday. The salesman said, "No, he is in the office today. I can better serve you, sir." My friend said, "No. He was very polite and went the extra mile to help me with the car and did not bother how I was dressed or whether I could afford it."

At that point, the owner of the showroom entered. "Everything alright?" he said. My friend said, "Yes, could you ask your young salesman to come out here please? I wish to buy the Ferrari he very nicely showed me yesterday, and he sold it to me in such a great manner and could not do enough for me." "Certainly," said the owner.

The young salesman came out with the owner, with the older salesman looking on, very miffed. My friend said, "Here is the cash in a plastic bag for the Ferrari." He said to the owner, "Make sure he gets his commission." The owner said. "He will. He is my son."

That young man will go a long way because he went the extra mile. That older salesman, on the other hand? My friend said his face was a picture. When you refuse to go the extra mile, you lose big-time in the end just like that.

So if you want more money, give more of yourself. The more you give unconditionally, the more you get back.

Can you remember when you used to go into a sweet shop and asked for a quarter of sweets? If you can't, then just imagine this, please.

You ask for a quarter of sweets. The lady gets the jar of sweets off the shelf and measures out the sweets on the scales. She looks at the scales and says, "I will put some more on there for you." How do you feel? Happy you have more than you asked for? You have more than you paid for. You are pleased.

Now imagine, how would you feel if they took some sweets off? When those sweets are on the scales, you believe they are yours. You get upset when the lady takes some off. Which lady went the extra mile? Where will you go for your sweets in future?

Just imagine, the biggest diamond in the world is under a paving slab in Oxford Street. There are over five thousand slabs. How many slabs would you lift up to look for that diamond?

Just five, and it would hurt your hands? Will you never be bothered?

No, you would rip up every slab as fast as you could. Fingers bleeding, back hurting, until you came to that diamond.

This is Nature's Power. Do the work first, then get your reward with belief.

***

Form a mastermind group with your partner, husband or wife. Remember that either your partner completes you or competes against you.

A shire horse can pull a ton. Two shire horses can pull three tons together. When you have a mastermind group, you are working together towards a goal.

Have mastermind meetings before you go to bed. When one is down, the other uplifts. Your partner is your greatest cheerleader. You are your partner's hero.

When a partner is fault-finding, nagging, indifferent to what the other is doing, this destroys success and happiness.

Look at a very successful football or rugby team. The greatest and the most successful are the ones that work together. They help and support each other. Work the space to allow their teammate to score. The greatest teams are the ones who use a mastermind group.

Marriage is the best mastermind group you can get and the most powerful.

With Nature's Power, there are things you need and things to avoid for it to work for your success. Some of the principles are:

- Get started today.
- Focus on your dream, major purpose, goal.
- Go the extra mile.
- Nourish your mastermind group.
- Act as if you already have your dream in your hand.

If I ask you to, how would you climb an oak tree? There are two ways:

Climbing up is hard work. You get scratched. You could fall and hurt yourself, but you keep going, getting tired, hurting, struggling, muscles getting weaker. You bang your head on the next branch. Hands bleeding, head wound, cut ear, torn nail, ripped trousers, a twig pokes you in the eye. Branch snaps as you put your foot on it, but you hang on as your goal is to get to the top. Hard work, you're hurting, bleeding, eye hurts, head hurts, and you're knackered. When you get to the top, all the pain and tiredness has gone.

The second way is to sit on an acorn and wait for it to grow. Which one is more practical? You know the answer yourself.

Don't delay. Start your incredible journey now.

An old Chinese proverb says:

The man who waits for a crispy duck to fly in his mouth waits a very long time.

Don't wait for all the lights to turn green. There is never a perfect time, but now.

***

Some reminders about Belief and Faith before reaching a close:

Everything in nature happens without thought. Everything happens because of nature. We, humans, are the only thing on this Earth who have been given a mind. A choice.

Spend time in nature. Go into the woods. Some trees have been there for hundreds of years. Their leaves appear in spring and fall in autumn. They drop their seeds and acorns to keep replenishing the trees. The sun and rain keep them going. Look at the birds, they naturally know when to migrate, when to build their nests. Look on the ground. The plants and bushes are all there for a reason. Insects know their job, so do the birds and animals - Nature does all this. All this keeps going well after we have gone. Look at the flowers, smell the scent they give off. They are all there for a reason, to attract the bees, to pollinate them and create more flowers.

The rivers ebb and flow through valleys and streams back to the ocean, cleansing as they go, the fish and the water plants. The sun and rain, day and night, over mountains and hills, all are following a system of nature. This is endless. It keeps on going all around the world with no mind or brain to direct it. Humans have been given a brain and two minds: the conscious and the subconscious. With these things, humans are superior, but how do we use these power? Some want to destroy the very trees and animals that follow the way of nature.

Nature's Power gave us a mind to think for ourselves. Not to rush around catching trains, buying cars, struggling to keep up with payments. When I bought my first house, we had no furniture, no holidays and an old van. Now people want a huge wedding which costs thousands, a brand-new house, all furnished, two holidays a year and two brand-new cars. They are living in the rat race, leaving home at 6 am and getting home at 8 pm because of heavy traffic or delayed trains. They want status, which means buying things they can't afford, to impress people they don't like. I know we must work to support ourselves, but not like a hamster in a wheel. We have been given a mind to work smart.

You see, the powerful people know how to use this power. They have got every country and its people into debt because they know that young people do not know delayed gratification. They want it now. They play straight into the hands of the powerful.

Do you want to work forty years in the rat race? I have never met a person who did this because they liked it. They do it for the money. They dread every Monday. Is this life? Is this what Nature's Power gives us a mind for? These people do not think. They are being used by people who use Nature's Power to the full.

If you are happy doing this and have a happy relationship, keep doing it. If not, stop. Do what you were put on this Earth to do. Everyone has been given a gift. You have been given a mind, which is the most powerful thing on Earth. It can attract anything you want. My life was only one example. Use these references to reflect on your own life, behaviours, patterns and events. Strengthen your intuition and faith. Do not listen to people's opinions. It is you who determines your future, nobody else.

Look at the bumblebee. People who understand aerodynamics say it is impossible for the bee to fly, but no one told the bumblebee. Everything in nature succeeds without a brain. We have been given one, hence we have to be more extraordinary than all other species. But most of us do not use it the way it was intended. Most use Nature's Power against themselves.

If you did not know about this power, congratulations, for now, you do. But this is still only the starting step.

Keep reading, keep listening. Believe in Nature's Power and start on your incredible journey for that happy life you always dreamt of. To take that dream to the next level, imagine having achieved that dream already. Belief and faith are powerful. You feed your body three times a day. Feed your mind positive thoughts every day, and live as you were intended to live.

Some final reminders before I let you go:

- Have a dream or major purpose or goal.
- Allow no time or space in mind for failure.
- Know where you are going before you start.
- Like planting a seed, know that your efforts will bear fruit.
- The best way to solve a challenge is to find someone with a worse challenge than yours and help them. By helping them, you will also solve yours.
- A dream or major purpose stops procrastination.
- Having a major purpose in your subconscious is a priceless asset, with a burning desire, a "rather die than lose" attitude.

Every man today is the result of his thoughts yesterday.
Belief backed by action can achieve anything you want.
Nature's power leads us to happiness, or to someone else's happiness.
If you don't determine your price, someone else will.

Joke

The police just pulled me over and said, "Papers?"

I said, "Scissors, I win," and drove off.

I think he wants a rematch - he's been chasing me for the last 45 minutes.

Your Notes

To all the people who read this book from the beginning to the end, read it again, dog-ear the book and mark the points which relate to you.

I love you all.

You are on the right road to your happiness.

You are riding life.

You are a player and not a spectator.

Hopefully, I will meet everybody who reads this book one day.

God bless.

- Gary